Tristan
D'Souza

War Machines written by: Christopher Maynard
Illustrated by: Derek Bunce, Wilfred Hardy, Dudley Moseley,
         Mike Roffe, Barry Rowe, Tony Simmonds

Aircraft written by: Christopher Tunney
Illustrated by: Simon Bishop, Wilfred Hardy, Mike Roffe, Ken Rush.

Designed by: Tri-Art
Series Editor: Christopher Tunney
Art Director: Keith Groom

**Published by Christensen Press Limited, The Grange,
Grange Yard, London SE1 3AG.
© Christensen Press Limited 1985**

**First published 1985
Revised edition 1990**

Printed and bound by Graficas Reunidas, Madrid, Spain.

ISBN: 0 946994 02 1

War Machines

Ⲫ Christensen Press

Have civilian vehicles a use in war?

BUSES TO MOTORCYCLES Modern warfare is not just a fight between professional armies. Warring countries use all their resources—civilian and military—in the struggle to defeat their enemies. In World Wars I and II, motorcycles, buses, cars, and trucks of every description operated in the battle areas.

At the outbreak of World War I in 1914, a large number of civilian Daimler motor buses were used to transport British Royal Marines to the fighting zones in France and Belgium. With their advertisements and their London destinations still showing, the buses were rushed to the front line. They stayed in the battle area for the rest of the war and were sometimes used for patrol work.

What are the smallest war vehicles?

As a means of giving parachute troops ground transport, small, collapsible motorcycles were invented. The two-stroke, single-cylinder *Parascooter* could fold into a canister and be dropped by parachute. It could travel at 30 mph (50 kph).

Are there any special battle motorcycles?

The *Kettenkraftrad* (treaded motorcycle) was a German invention that was half motorcycle and half tractor. It was designed to provide parachute units with a light but powerful vehicle, and was first used successfully during the airborne invasion of Crete in 1941. It could carry two passengers or tow light guns, and had a top speed of about 50 mph (80 kph).

What popular car began life as a war machine?

The *Kubelwagen*, the most widely used German small reconnaissance car of World War II, was derived from an early version of the famous Volkswagen "Beetle." It had the same air-cooled rear engine and suspension, but a simple, box-like body. It was light and easily handled, and had an excellent cross-country performance.

The rear-engined *Kubelwagen* was light and tough.

What is the most adaptable war vehicle?

TRUCKS BIG AND SMALL Trucks play a vital role in war. Usually, they are the only means by which supplies can be moved up to the battlefront. In war zones, supply trucks are sometimes armed with guns and sent in convoys for safety. But trucks have many uses apart from supply. Some carry troops. Others act as tractors, and tow guns or broken-down vehicles. Special-purpose trucks fulfill such functions as carrying fuel and fighting fires.

The "blitz buggy" was an early name for the jeep, the most famous vehicle of World War II. Nearly 640,000 jeeps were built between December, 1941 and the end of the war. Officially, the jeep was described as a "$\frac{1}{4}$-ton truck with 4-wheel drive". Its many uses became legendary: everything from reconnaissance to towing light guns and carrying wounded soldiers.

The jeep was probably World War II's most adaptable vehicle.

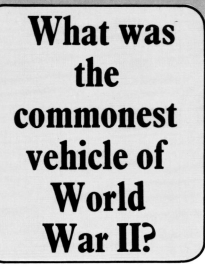

What was the commonest vehicle of World War II?

The American 2$\frac{1}{2}$-ton truck was seen on many battle fronts.

More than 800,000 American 2$\frac{1}{2}$-ton trucks were made during the war. Because of their 6-wheel drive, these trucks handled well, both on and off the road. Aside from being general cargo carriers, they had many other uses—as dumpers, for example, and as tankers.

What are the heaviest battle loads?

One of the heaviest loads in war is a tank. A big battle tank can weigh 50 tons or more. Special tractor-trailers of immense power are used to haul such huge loads.

Tank transporters assist the recovery of damaged tanks.

Do trucks have any unusual war uses?

Track-laying trucks provide strong "instant" roads.

Military trucks are called on to do many unusual jobs. One such task is the laying of a portable road. A long strip of flexible metal "planking" is carried on a large spool on the truck's platform. The strip is unrolled to form a roadway for vehicles across soft-surfaced land, such as a beach.

What special trucks do armies use?

Military fire-fighting vehicle

Fast fire engines are used by military units in depots and airfields. The vehicles are designed for travel across rough country where necessary. The one shown here has two tanks, one containing foam mixture, the other water. It produces and projects foam to blanket fires. Where explosives or inflammable liquids are stored, fires can quickly become disastrous.

What is an amphibian?

SWIMMERS AND WADERS In modern warfare, armies have to be able to move almost anywhere, overcoming the most varied obstacles. Foremost among these are water obstacles—rivers, lakes, or even seas. Many types of vehicles have been invented that can move swiftly from land into the water without delaying operations. Some such machines are swimmers or amphibians. Others are simply waders that travel underwater by crawling along the bottom.

An amphibian is a craft that is equally at home on land and in the water. A good example was the Russian K-61 personnel carrier. This tracked vehicle could move at 22 mph (36 kph) on land. In the water, even fully loaded, it could manage 6 mph (10 kph), driven by twin propellers. The K-61 could carry 32 troops in its open-top hull, and had a three-man crew.

The Russian K-61 was designed with tracks and propellers.

Do amphibians need harbors?

The DUKW had wheels and a propeller.

The LVT4 used its tracks for propulsion on land and water.

Seaborne landings along coastlines often take place far from harbors. The invading force is off-loaded from large ships into landing craft and amphibious vehicles for the run to the shore. The American LVT4 was a tracked amphibian of World War II. Up to 30 men could be carried in its boat-like hull. The DUKW was an amphibious wheeled truck. It swam to the shore driven by a propeller, then drove across the beach and onto the roads.

How are land vehicles made to swim?

The amphibious jeep included an anchor in its equipment.

By replacing the standard jeep body with a boat-like hull, this small vehicle could be transformed into an amphibian. Once it was in the water, the propeller was powered by the same drive that turned the wheels. This swimming vehicle had the same performance on land as any other jeep.

Below : Ka-Chi amphibious tank with detachable wooden pontoons at front and rear. In water, it was driven by propellers.

Below right : Sherman tank fitted with a folding canvas "boat" that enabled it to swim.

Are any vehicles too heavy to swim?

Light and medium tanks, such as the Japanese *Ka-Chi* and the American *Sherman* will float by adding pontoons or raised canvas screens that give extra buoyancy. But heavy tanks have to be turned into waders by waterproofing. Using a long tube-like "snorkel," a waterproofed tank can breathe as it wades across the bottom of a river or crawls up a beach.

Tank fitted with "snorkel" device for beach landing or crossing water obstacles.

What is a caterpillar tread?

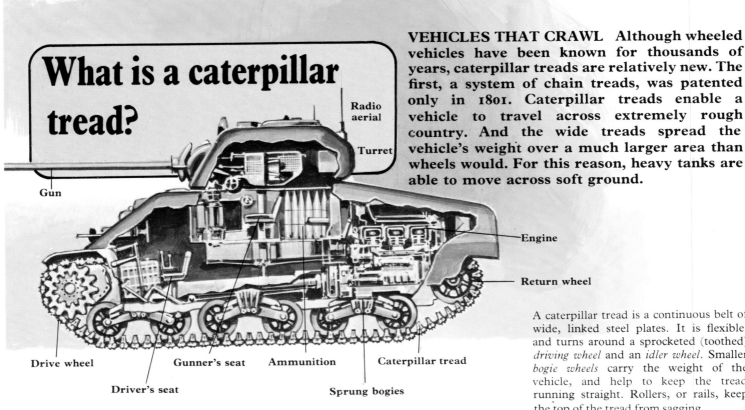

- Radio aerial
- Turret
- Gun
- Engine
- Return wheel
- Drive wheel
- Gunner's seat
- Ammunition
- Caterpillar tread
- Driver's seat
- Sprung bogies

VEHICLES THAT CRAWL Although wheeled vehicles have been known for thousands of years, caterpillar treads are relatively new. The first, a system of chain treads, was patented only in 1801. Caterpillar treads enable a vehicle to travel across extremely rough country. And the wide treads spread the vehicle's weight over a much larger area than wheels would. For this reason, heavy tanks are able to move across soft ground.

A caterpillar tread is a continuous belt of wide, linked steel plates. It is flexible, and turns around a sprocketed (toothed) *driving wheel* and an *idler wheel*. Smaller *bogie wheels* carry the weight of the vehicle, and help to keep the tread running straight. Rollers, or rails, keep the top of the tread from sagging.

How were treaded vehicles first used in war?

Holt gas-driven farm tractor

The first effective use of treaded machines was in World War I when the Holt steam tractor—a farming machine—was put to work towing heavy artillery. This large half-track was used by French and British units to pull field guns and howitzers, because it was the only vehicle capable of moving over the churned-up ground of the battlefront.

What disadvantages had early caterpillar treads?

The Mulus

Early caterpillar vehicles were slow-moving, and their treads had a short working life. The Austrians solved this problem with their highly original A.D.M.K. *Mulus* (Mule) of 1935. By lowering its road wheels, it could be converted from a treaded vehicle to a wheeled one.

What are half-treads?

These are vehicles that manage to combine some of the sturdy cross-country performance of tanks with armored cars' ability to move swiftly on roads. The most common half-tread of World War II was the German SdKfz 7; more than 3,000 were built. This heavy machine worked as a troop carrier and gun tractor. Its top speed was about 30 mph (50 kph).

The SdKfz 7 was driven by its treads.

Are tanks the only fully treaded vehicles?

The M6 high-speed tractor towed heavy guns.

As tread life improved and speeds increased, more and more fighting machines were switched from wheels to treads. A good example of a fully treaded World War II vehicle that was not a tank was the American M6 high-speed tractor. It was able to drag heavy guns across rough country at a speed equal to that of a tank.

What were the first armored cars like?

When the Austro-Daimler armored car appeared in 1903, it was hailed as a triumph. It was the first machine of its kind to have the armor as part of its structure. Earlier armored cars had merely had sheets of steel bolted on for protection. The Austro-Daimler also had a swivelling turret carrying a machine gun.

Austro-Daimler armored car

ARMOR FOR DEFENSE AND ATTACK
Armored vehicles of many kinds are essential in modern land warfare. These vehicles are bullet proof to small-caliber fire and, when mounted with guns, can also fight in their own right. Armored cars are used for liaison and reconnaissance work, and take part in cross-country operations. Armored troop carrier ferry men and equipment into the thick of the fighting.

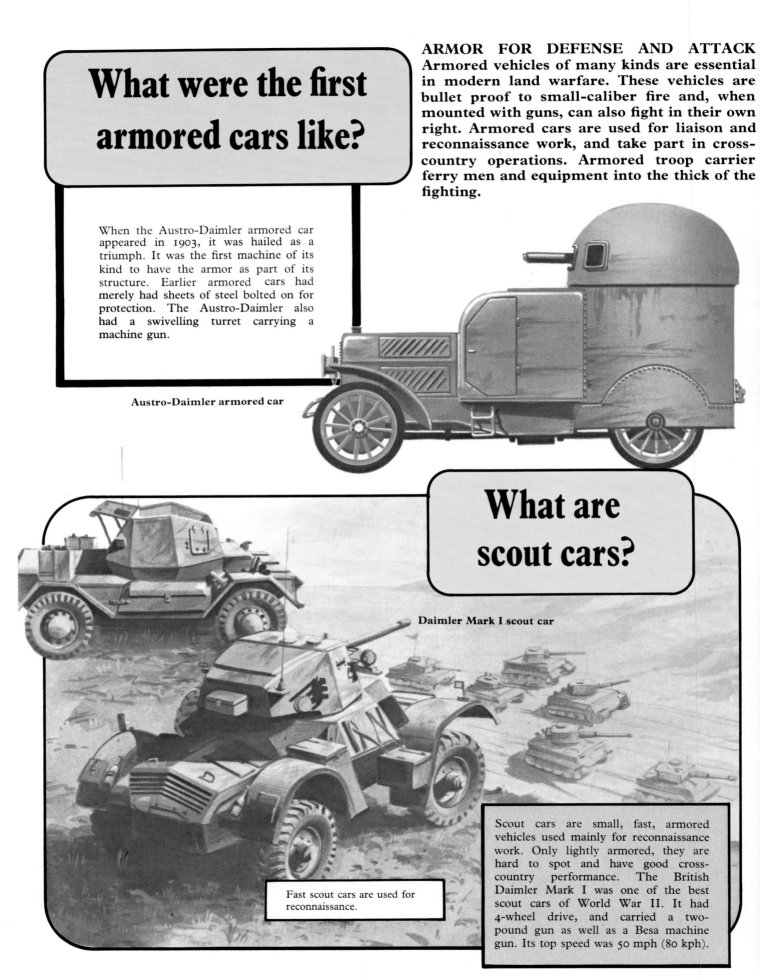

What are scout cars?

Daimler Mark I scout car

Fast scout cars are used for reconnaissance.

Scout cars are small, fast, armored vehicles used mainly for reconnaissance work. Only lightly armored, they are hard to spot and have good cross-country performance. The British Daimler Mark I was one of the best scout cars of World War II. It had 4-wheel drive, and carried a two-pound gun as well as a Besa machine gun. Its top speed was 50 mph (80 kph).

Are armored cars used in attack?

Puma heavy armored car

The German SdKfz 234/2 *Puma* of World War II, though mainly a reconnaissance car, would occasionally attack small tanks. This 8-wheeler carried a 50 mm gun and a machine gun in its enclosed turret. It had a range of about 500 miles (800 km) and a top speed of 53 mph (85 kph). It had a crew of four.

What was a "battle taxi"?

The "battle taxi" was the nickname given to the British *Universal Carrier*. It was a light, tracked vehicle, and had many uses and many versions. Generally, it was used as a personnel carrier. But sometimes it was armed with a machine gun, or even with a two-pound gun or a mortar. More than 70,000 carriers were built.

Several countries have personnel carriers that can operate on land or water. In the 1960's, the Russian army put the BTR-60P armored carrier into service. This 8-wheeled vehicle can carry a large body of troops across water obstacles, and can work equally well cross-country and on roads. It has an open-top armored hull.

An Armored Carrier That Swims

Russian amphibious armored carrier

Is the tank a modern invention?

BATTLESHIPS OF THE LAND For the fighting men inside it, a tank is a mobile fortress. It was a revolutionary weapon when it was first used in battle in World War I. It combined firepower, mobility, and protection in a single unit in a way no other vehicle had achieved. Its effect was devastating, because it was the first weapon capable of ending the stalemate of trench warfare.

The idea of the tank goes back hundreds of years. The thought of an armored, gun-bearing, mobile fortress has always appealed to soldiers. But the problem of powering such a machine was difficult to solve. Early attèmpts to propel "tanks" with horses and steam engines were unsuccessful. Only with the invention of the gas engine was an answer found.

German wooden mobile fortress of the 1500's.

Mobile pill box.

Design for a steam-propelled tank.

Design for a steam-propelled land dreadnaught.

When were tanks first used in battle?

The tank was able to force its way over the dreaded barbed-wire of the Western Front.

Tanks were first used in action during the Battle of the Somme in 1916. But their success was limited because of mud. The big breakthrough came at Cambrai in the following year, when 300 British tanks breached the enemy lines, and advanced 4 miles (6 km) into the enemy positions.

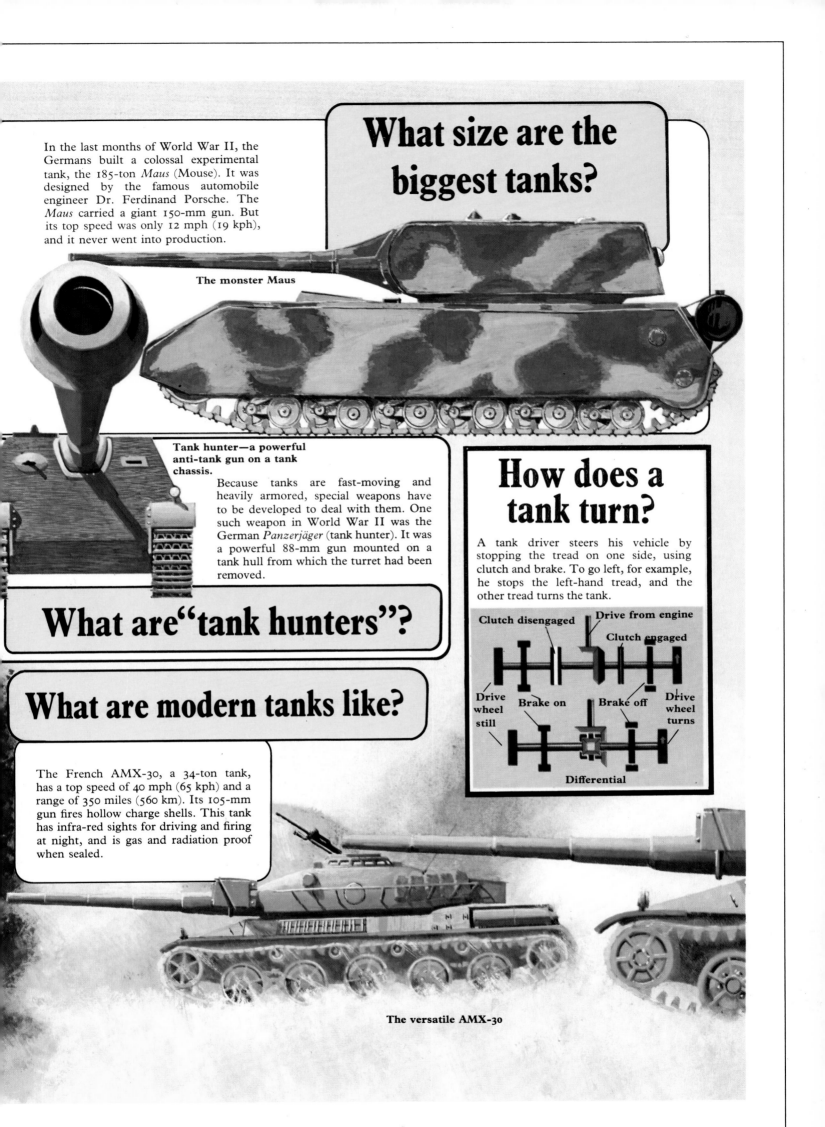

What size are the biggest tanks?

In the last months of World War II, the Germans built a colossal experimental tank, the 185-ton *Maus* (Mouse). It was designed by the famous automobile engineer Dr. Ferdinand Porsche. The *Maus* carried a giant 150-mm gun. But its top speed was only 12 mph (19 kph), and it never went into production.

The monster Maus

Tank hunter—a powerful anti-tank gun on a tank chassis.

What are "tank hunters"?

Because tanks are fast-moving and heavily armored, special weapons have to be developed to deal with them. One such weapon in World War II was the German *Panzerjäger* (tank hunter). It was a powerful 88-mm gun mounted on a tank hull from which the turret had been removed.

How does a tank turn?

A tank driver steers his vehicle by stopping the tread on one side, using clutch and brake. To go left, for example, he stops the left-hand tread, and the other tread turns the tank.

Clutch disengaged | Drive from engine | Clutch engaged

Drive wheel still | Brake on | Brake off | Drive wheel turns

Differential

What are modern tanks like?

The French AMX-30, a 34-ton tank, has a top speed of 40 mph (65 kph) and a range of 350 miles (560 km). Its 105-mm gun fires hollow charge shells. This tank has infra-red sights for driving and firing at night, and is gas and radiation proof when sealed.

The versatile AMX-30

What were battlefront railroads?

RAILROADS AT WAR Railroads play a vital part in modern warfare. They are the single most effective way of transporting the vast numbers of men and the mountains of material needed. And they enable armies to draw on reserves often located hundreds of miles from the main fighting. But railroads are highly vulnerable targets for bombing and sabotage. All armies have to keep trained engineers ready to repair damaged lines and rolling stock.

Narrow 2-foot gauge railroads were built in World War I to supply depots and hospitals just behind the front line. The track foundations needed little preparation because locomotives and cars were light. The track was easily repaired when damaged by shelling. The most common locomotive was the Baldwin 4-6-oT.

How have war-zone trains been protected?

Railroads are always open to hit-and-run attacks, especially where lines of communication are long, such as in Russia in World War II. The locomotive shown here is shielded by a massive box of armor plate. The cars each carry a rapid-firing gun mounted in an armored turret.

Do railroads have many uses in war?

British hospital trains used converted railroad cars, fitted to carry 6 to 12 stretchers as well as seated casualties. Drewry "B" motor ambulance trolley carried 4 stretchers. They were self-powered cars with controls at each end.

Armored train, draped in steel plating.

The 600-mm mortar gun "Karl" of World War II was the largest treaded vehicle of the war. It weighed 120 tons. When it was moved by train, two cars were needed to carry it. Its 37-foot (11-meter) length was slung between the cars, and in this way the enormous load was pulled carefully along.

What are the biggest loads they have carried?

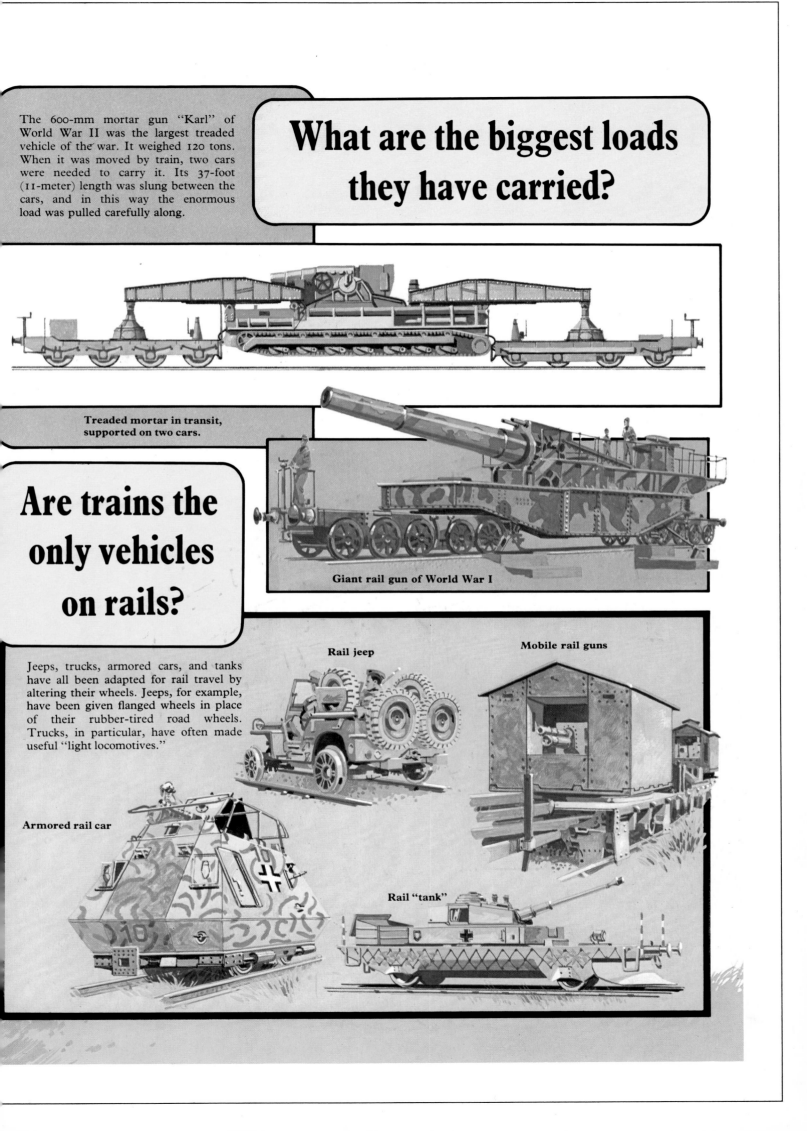

Treaded mortar in transit, supported on two cars.

Giant rail gun of World War I

Are trains the only vehicles on rails?

Jeeps, trucks, armored cars, and tanks have all been adapted for rail travel by altering their wheels. Jeeps, for example, have been given flanged wheels in place of their rubber-tired road wheels. Trucks, in particular, have often made useful "light locomotives."

Rail jeep

Mobile rail guns

Armored rail car

Rail "tank"

When were military helicopters first used?

THE HELICOPTER JOINS IN Helicopters cannot fly as fast or as high as fixed-wing planes, but they are far more maneuverable. They are used by all modern armies. Helicopters are ideal for reconnaissance and transport. They can drop troops into the heart of battle, carry wounded to safety, and transport supplies to isolated positions. They also have a fighting role, chiefly as fast gunships.

In World War II, the German navy successfully put a helicopter into use. The Flettner· *Kolibri* (Hummingbird) was a tiny open-cockpit machine used for patrol work. It first went into service in 1942. With a range of 100 miles (160 km) and a speed of 95 mph (150 kph), it provided a much-needed extra set of eyes for large warships.

Flettner FL 282B Kolibri

Why are helicopters used for rescue work?

Bell SRR/222

Unlike other planes, helicopters can fly in almost any direction, and can land and take off nearly anywhere. They can also hover in the air—a capability that makes them perfect for rescue work. In sea rescues, they often use a winch to reach people in the water and to lift them to safety.

What other special uses do they have?

CCCP·04102

Helicopters that are built to carry heavy loads under the fuselage are called "flying cranes." The Russian Mil Mi-10 can even lift a heavy vehicle on the platform fitted between its long, giraffe-like legs. Up to 28 people can ride in the cabin above.

Mil Mi-10

How far can they fly?

Like all helicopters, the Sikorsky HH-3E, or "Jolly Green Giant," has a short range compared to winged planes. Yet two HH-3Es set a record for non-stop travel in 1967 when they flew 4,270 miles (6,870 km) across the North Atlantic. It took nine mid-air refuellings to get them over.

Helicopters have grown to truly gigantic sizes since the earliest models. The Russian Mil Mi-12, a four-engined monster, is 121 feet (37 meters) long. It is larger than many heavy transport airplanes. One of the smallest helicopters is the American Hughes OH-6A *Cayuse*, which is only 21 feet (6.5 meters) long.

How big are helicopters compared with other planes?

Mil Mi-12

ДЭРОФЛОТ

CCCP-21142

H-833

Large and small helicopters drawn to scale—compared with a man and a medium-sized transport plane.

Hughes OH-6A Cayuse

ARMY

192

ROYAL AIR FORCE

XV192

192

Lockheed C-130 Hercules transport plane

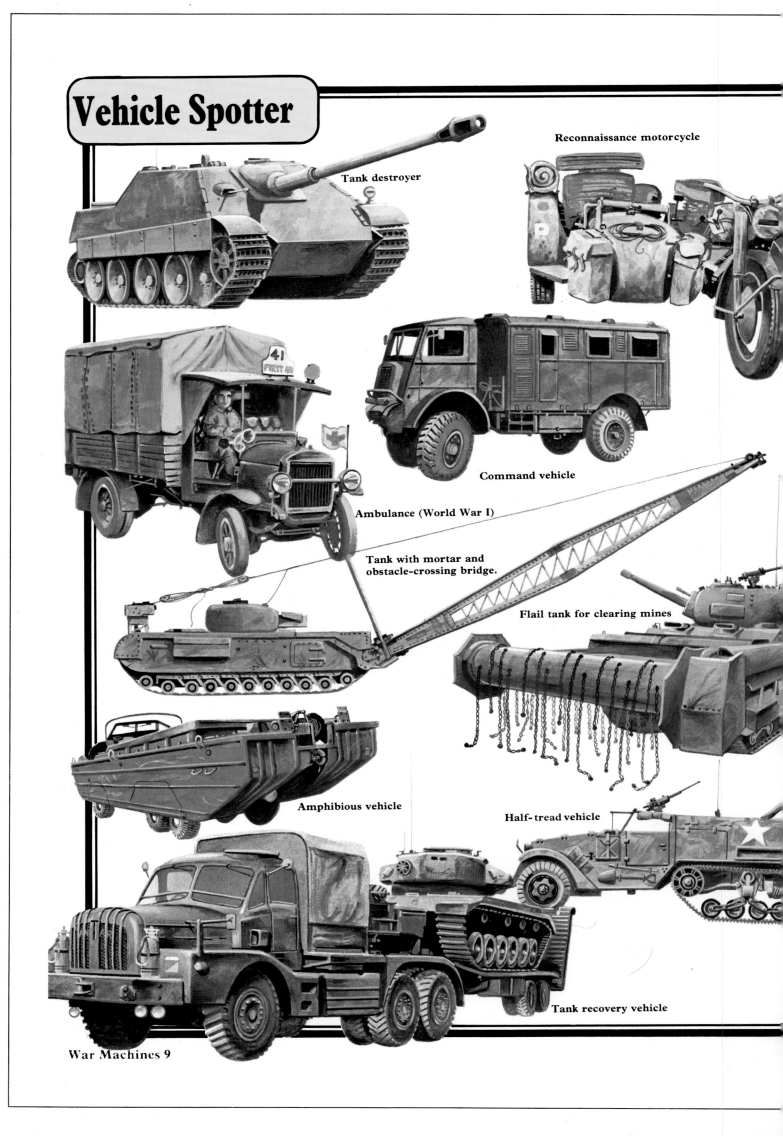

Vehicle Spotter

Tank destroyer

Reconnaissance motorcycle

Command vehicle

Ambulance (World War I)

Tank with mortar and obstacle-crossing bridge.

Flail tank for clearing mines

Amphibious vehicle

Half-tread vehicle

Tank recovery vehicle

War Machines 9

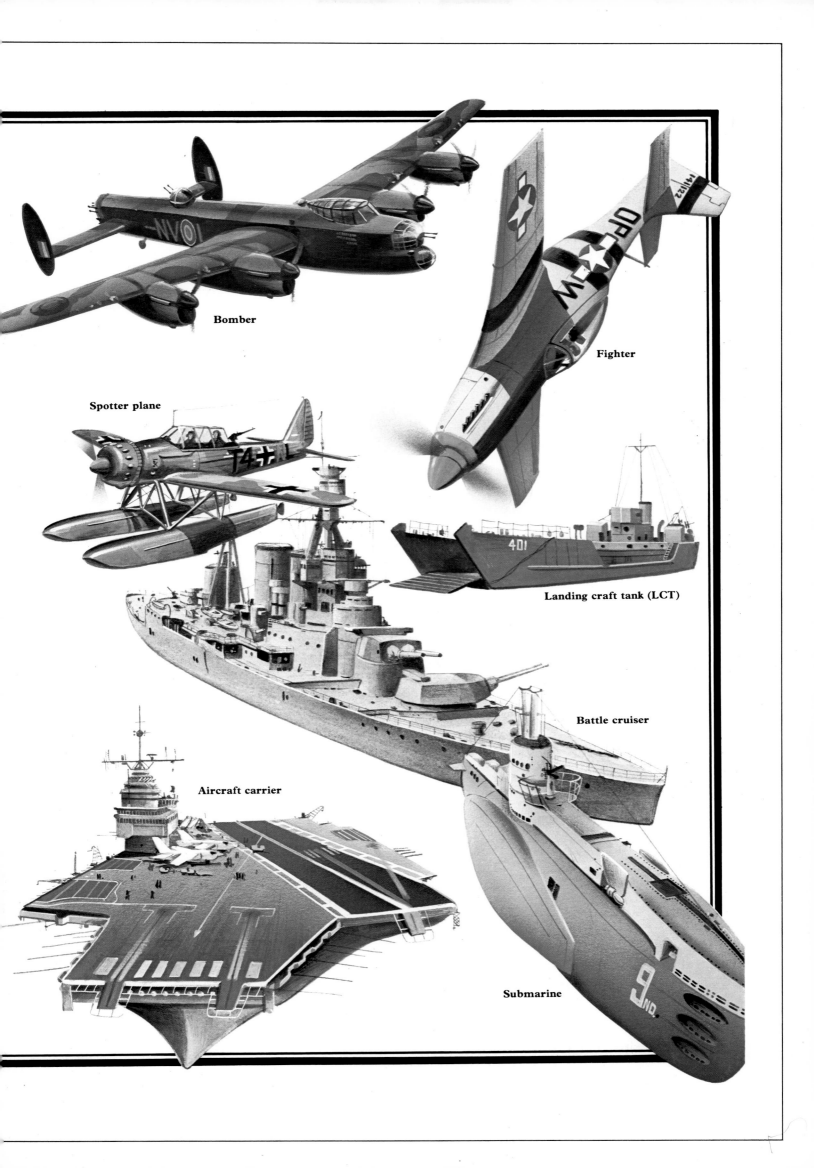

Bomber

Fighter

Spotter plane

Landing craft tank (LCT)

Battle cruiser

Aircraft carrier

Submarine

Who first landed an airplane on a ship?

FLOATING AIRPORTS Aircraft carriers are the largest warships in modern navies. They are also the most important ships, because they enable the tremendous striking-power of aircraft to be carried into enemy territory, no matter how distant it may be. During World War II, some of the greatest naval battles were in fact air battles, fought by airplanes from the carriers of opposing naval fleets.

Eugene Ely lands on USS Pennsylvania

The first ship landing took place in January, 1911, when Eugene Ely landed a Curtiss biplane on a specially built platform on the USS *Pennsylvania*. In August, 1917, Squadron Commander E. H. Dunning landed a Sopwith biplane on the deck of a moving ship, HMS *Furious*.

E. H. Dunning lands on HMS Furious

What does a modern aircraft carrier look like?

Island

Bridge

Arrester wire

Elevator

Flight deck

Whip aerials

The aircraft carrier is a floating air base. Its deck is an airfield. Part of the deck is at an angle to the main axis of the ship, and forms the runway on which planes land. The ship is controlled from the *island* or *superstructure*, which is not only the captain's bridge but is also the control tower. Elevators move planes from the flight deck to their hangars below.

What is a carrier like inside?

Below its flight deck, a carrier has hangar decks in which the planes are stored when not in use. It also has repair shops, storage space for ammunition and fuel, and living quarters for the crew.

Hangar

Service hangar

Turbines

Service shops, store rooms, etc.

Fuel tanks

What other ships carry aircraft in war?

Spotter plane acting as "eyes" for cruiser

Cruiser

Unarmed merchantman

Armed merchant ship with catapult plane

Many warships carry aircraft—either airplanes or helicopters—to act as their "eyes." Such spotter aircraft are particularly useful in war both for locating enemy convoys and for convoy protection. During World War II, some merchant ships carried planes that could be catapulted from their decks. On completion of his mission, the pilot had to ditch his plane in the sea and wait to be picked up.

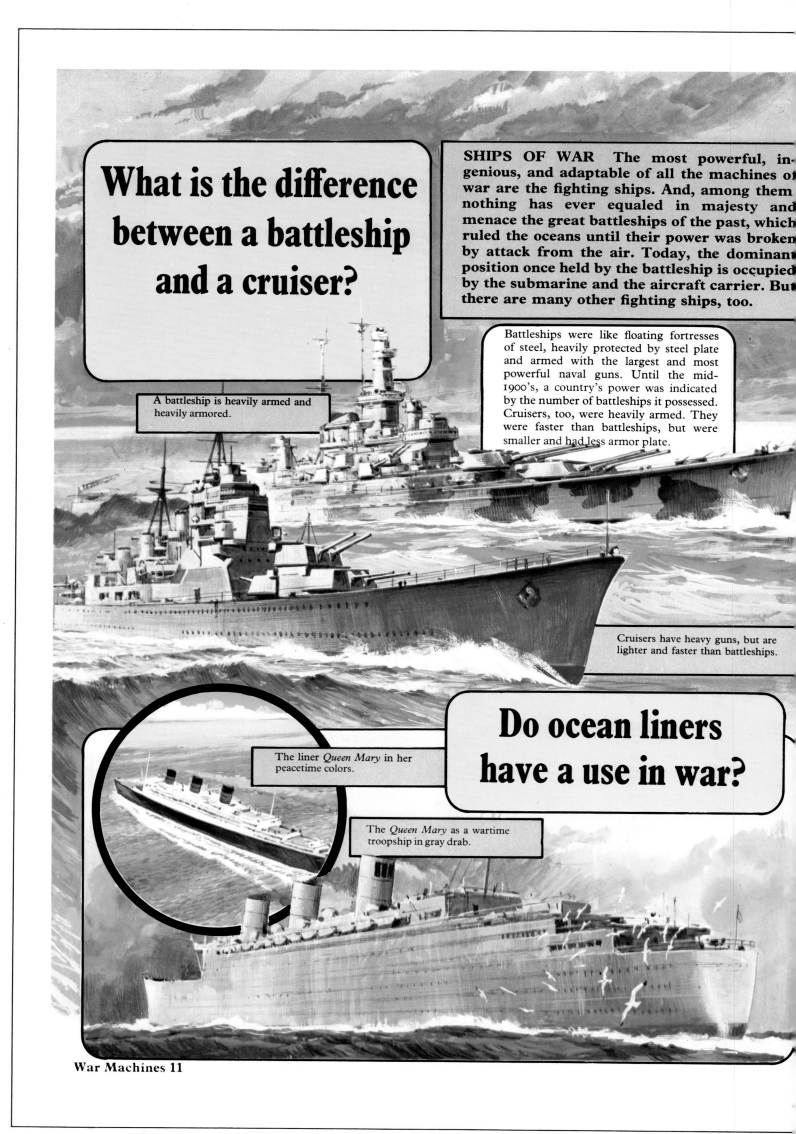

What is the difference between a battleship and a cruiser?

SHIPS OF WAR The most powerful, ingenious, and adaptable of all the machines of war are the fighting ships. And, among them nothing has ever equaled in majesty and menace the great battleships of the past, which ruled the oceans until their power was broken by attack from the air. Today, the dominant position once held by the battleship is occupied by the submarine and the aircraft carrier. But there are many other fighting ships, too.

Battleships were like floating fortresses of steel, heavily protected by steel plate and armed with the largest and most powerful naval guns. Until the mid-1900's, a country's power was indicated by the number of battleships it possessed. Cruisers, too, were heavily armed. They were faster than battleships, but were smaller and had less armor plate.

A battleship is heavily armed and heavily armored.

Cruisers have heavy guns, but are lighter and faster than battleships.

Do ocean liners have a use in war?

The liner *Queen Mary* in her peacetime colors.

The *Queen Mary* as a wartime troopship in gray drab.

Why is the submarine so feared?

U-boat hunts its victims.

The invention of the submarine changed naval warfare. Other warships —surface vessels—could not easily detect the presence of the hidden enemy who sailed right up to them under-water, and then fired its deadly tor-pedoes. Today, the submarine can sail close to enemy territory and launch long-range missiles against land targets.

Two-man "human torpedoes" had many successes.

Nuclear submarines can travel great distances on ocean patrols.

Submarine surfaces at night on an empty sea.

Midget submarines carried external torpedoes.

Life on a submarine is cramped and uncomfortable. Often, the air is heavy and humid. In war, submarine crews face extreme danger as well as discomfort. For this reason, submarine sailors in most navies are all volunteers and are carefully selected.

What is life like in a submarine?

Officers' wardroom

Diving control center

How did the convoy system work?

Instead of making a lone voyage, a loaded cargo ship waited in a safe port until several other ships were also ready to sail for the same destination. The group of ships then set out together as a "convoy." They were protected by an escort of armed naval ships. The convoy stayed together throughout the voyage. It could only sail as fast as the slowest ship in it.

CONVOYS FOR SAFETY The all-out attack by German submarines on Allied shipping in the last years of World War I was a new and terrible kind of warfare that produced astonishing results. Between February and April, 1917, 800 merchant ships were sunk. If such losses had continued, Britain might well have been starved into defeat because much of its food was imported by sea. To protect merchant ships against the submarine menace, the convoy system was developed.

How were the ships organized?

The merchant ships were herded in a tight rectangle made up of several columns of vessels. Each ship had its "station"—a position at a certain distance from each of its neighbors. It stayed in this station throughout the voyage. Naval ships formed a protecting escort screen around the convoy. They kept a constant watch for enemy aircraft, surface ships, and submarines.

Escorting warships

Merchant ships

Who protected them?

Many escort carriers were converted merchant ships.

Fast destroyers hunted enemy submarines and surface ships.

Corvettes were the smallest ships used as escorts.

Several kinds of naval vessels were used to shepherd convoys from port to port. They included cruisers, destroyers, frigates, corvettes, aircraft carriers, and minesweepers. They were armed with guns, torpedoes, and depth charges. And they used sonar, radar, and high-frequency direction-finding equipment to locate enemy vessels.

Were merchant ships ever armed?

During World War II, many merchant ships were equipped with guns. For example, Liberty ships (the wartime merchant vessels mass-produced in the United States) often carried 4-inch guns fore and aft, and some quick-firing anti-aircraft guns near the bridge. But their armament was of little use against warships.

What was degaussing?

Degaussing was a protection against magnetic mines. These mines exploded when they entered the magnetic field of a passing ship. But when a degaussing "girdle" was fitted round a ship and electric current was fed to it, the mines were made harmless. Waves of electric current from the girdle neutralized the magnetic field.

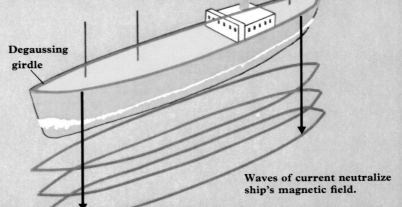

Degaussing girdle

Waves of current neutralize ship's magnetic field.

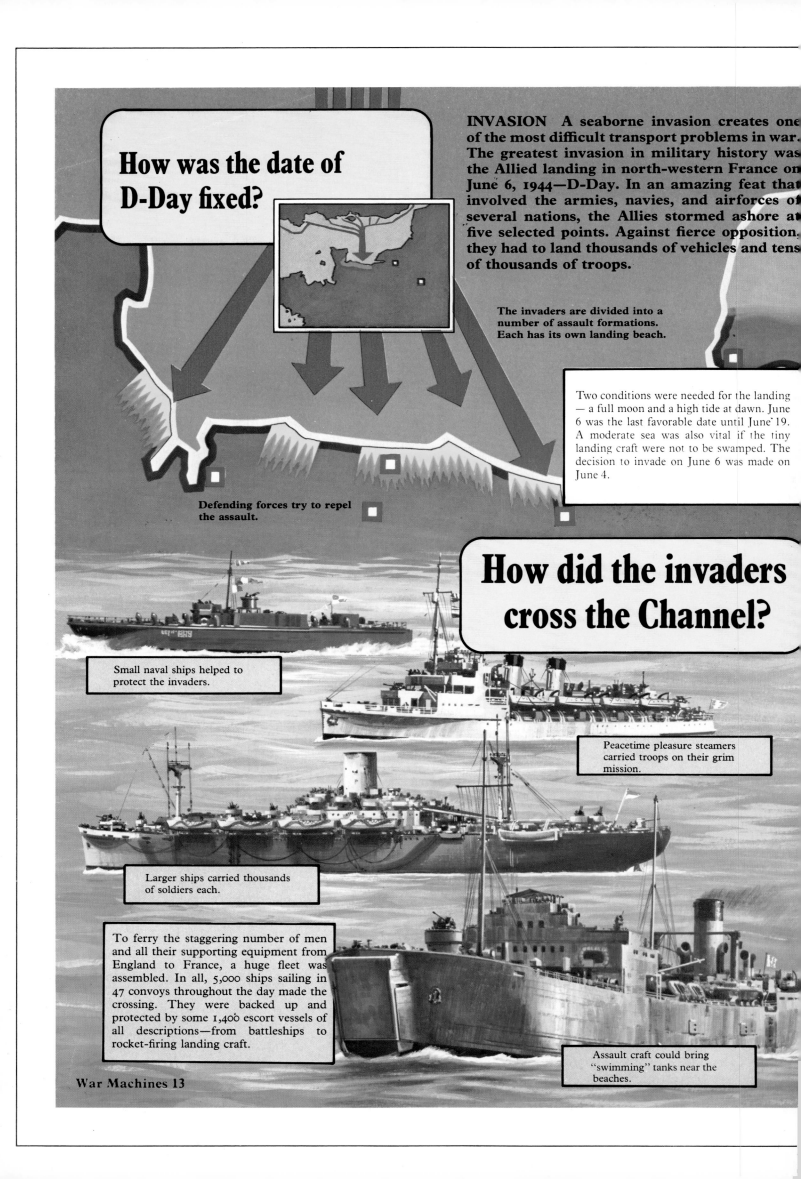

How was the date of D-Day fixed?

INVASION A seaborne invasion creates one of the most difficult transport problems in war. The greatest invasion in military history was the Allied landing in north-western France on June 6, 1944—D-Day. In an amazing feat that involved the armies, navies, and airforces of several nations, the Allies stormed ashore at five selected points. Against fierce opposition, they had to land thousands of vehicles and tens of thousands of troops.

The invaders are divided into a number of assault formations. Each has its own landing beach.

Two conditions were needed for the landing — a full moon and a high tide at dawn. June 6 was the last favorable date until June 19. A moderate sea was also vital if the tiny landing craft were not to be swamped. The decision to invade on June 6 was made on June 4.

Defending forces try to repel the assault.

How did the invaders cross the Channel?

Small naval ships helped to protect the invaders.

Peacetime pleasure steamers carried troops on their grim mission.

Larger ships carried thousands of soldiers each.

To ferry the staggering number of men and all their supporting equipment from England to France, a huge fleet was assembled. In all, 5,000 ships sailing in 47 convoys throughout the day made the crossing. They were backed up and protected by some 1,400 escort vessels of all descriptions—from battleships to rocket-firing landing craft.

Assault craft could bring "swimming" tanks near the beaches.

How did they land?

LCMs deposited road vehicles and light tanks on the shore.

The shelving coast made it impossible for large ships to come close inshore. To get ashore, men and vehicles had to be transferred to some 4,000 smaller landing craft for the run to the beach. Water-proofed vehicles drove out of the landing craft and through shallow water onto dry land.

LCAs ferried troops ashore from larger craft.

LCTs brought tanks and troops right to the beaches.

How many men and machines were involved?

The scale of the D-Day landing was gigantic. The plans called for 1,500 tanks, 5,000 other treaded fighting vehicles, 3,000 big guns, and 10,500 other machines from jeeps to bulldozers to come ashore on the first day. With them came 176,000 fighting men.

Tank carrying "fascine" to bridge anti-tank ditches

Flail tank

Tank with collapsible swimming-screen

Bridgelayer tank

Many types of armored vehicles take part in an invasion.

Tank hull with bridge ramps

Miniature Driverless Tank

STRANGE VEHICLES In the race to gain military superiority, armies have toyed with very odd ideas and very strange vehicles. In the 20th century, more than ever before, war has been a struggle of machines. The catalogue of strange fighting contraptions ranges from inspired notions born on the battlefield to feats of military engineering carefully thought out and painstakingly put into effect.

The *Goliath*, a miniature, driverless tank, was developed by the Germans in World War II. Just over knee-high, it carried a load of 220 lb (100 kg) of high explosive. The *Goliath* was used to attack well-defended positions, fortifications, and ordinary tanks. It was driven by battery-powered electric motors, and directed by radio.

The Russian KT vehicle was produced experimentally as a means of using a light T-60 tank in airborne attacks. The tank, which weighed 6 tons, was fitted with biplane wings, twin tail booms, and a tail mounting—all in wood. It was towed into the air, and was then released into battle as a glider.

Tank That Took to the Air

Car with Skis and Propeller

The heavy winter snows of the Russian front severely hampered the German army in World War II. One solution to finding a machine that could travel through deep snow was an experimental "ski-car." The body of a Tatra 87 car was mounted on skis. The front skis could be swivelled to steer the vehicle. A wide rear drive-wheel and propeller provided the drive.

Church on Wheels

Standard army vehicles have been converted for the most unlikely uses. One example was a mobile church used by the British army during its campaign in the desert of North Africa. An old 3-ton, 6-wheeled truck was given a new wooden body. The chaplain lived in an "apartment" in front, and held outdoor services from the altar at the back.

The Pedaling Machine-Gunner

Early bicycles had few obvious military uses for which horses or cars would not be better. But motorcycles were another thing. Several inventors tried to turn them into light attack machines. One of the earliest of such inventions was the Simms 4-wheel motorcycle of 1898. It mounted a Maxim machine gun and a thin armor shield. The gentleman who demonstrated this new weapon of war did little to strike terror into the enemy.

A New Method of Propulsion

A very original idea for a vehicle that could go where other machines would bog down was the Chrysler *Marsh Amphibian* of 1965. Able to cross mud, snow, and marshy ground, it consisted of a box-like hull mounted on two screw-threaded cylinders. The turning cylinders drove the machine forward.

A-Z of
War Vehicles

A

AA gun Abbreviation for *anti-aircraft gun*. AA guns were small-caliber, quick-firing weapons, sometimes mounted in pairs or clusters. The Bofors gun, a Swedish 40 mm, was widely used in World War II.

aircraft carrier A ship designed to carry and launch planes at sea. It acts as a floating airdrome.

amphibian Any vehicle that has the ability to travel both on land and on water.

anti-tank gun A light field gun that is easy to tow around the battle area, and can fire armor-piercing shells to stop tanks. Anti-tank guns may be mounted on treaded vehicles, and used as tank hunters.

APC Abbreviation for *armored personnel carrier*. Such vehicles may be treaded or wheeled, and are used to ferry troops into battle.

armor Plates of toughened steel used to protect tanks and other fighting vehicles from gunfire. Armor is often sloped to help deflect shells.

armored car A small, lightly armored vehicle used mainly for scouting. Such machines are swift, and can often travel cross-country.

artillery General term for such heavy weapons as field guns, anti-aircraft guns, and large mortars.

asdic An anti-submarine detecting device. *See* SONAR.

B

barrage Sustained fire by a large number of field guns. Often, the purpose of a barrage is to swamp an enemy strongpoint with fire in preparation for an attack by infantry. In World War I, a heavy barrage, often lasting for days, might consume millions of rounds.

Battle of the Somme During this battle on the Western Front in 1916, tanks were used in war for the first time. But they had only limited success because of badly churned-up ground and poor tactics.

bazooka An American anti-tank weapon of World War II, the bazooka fired a small rocket able to stop tanks at short range. This light, portable weapon enabled infantry units to defend themselves against tanks.

bhp Abbreviation for *brake horsepower*. This term describes the actual horsepower exerted by an engine.

Blitzkrieg German word meaning *lightning war*. This method of attack was developed in World War II as a way of avoiding the stalemate tactics of World War I. It combined dive-bomber attacks with concentrations of rapidly moving armored columns. The armor was followed by motorized infantry and mobile artillery units. The idea was to smash a hole in the enemy front line, then pour through and spread chaos behind the lines. The opposing army was broken up into small, easily defeated fragments.

bogie wheels The row of wheels that carry a tank's weight on its tracks.

booby traps Hidden devices filled with explosives and used to make fields, roads, and beaches treacherous for advancing troops.

bren gun A light, hand-held machine gun used by British troops in World War II.

Buffalo The name used in the British Army for the LVT 4, an American amphibious treaded vehicle able to carry up to 30 men.

C

caliber The size of a bullet or shell as measured by its diameter.

Cambrai The site of an important battle in World War I where, in November, 1917, tanks proved their effectiveness in war. Some 300 British tanks smashed through the German lines for a distance of 4 miles (6 km).

camouflage The colors and patterns with which fighting equipment is painted in order to make it difficult to spot. The aim is to make the equipment blend into its background.

catapult A machine on the flight deck of an aircraft carrier or some other ship, used to hurl planes into the air at high speed and so assist their take-off.

caterpillar treads A continuous belt of linked metal plates used by tanks and many other vehicles as a means of movement. Treads give much better cross-country performance than wheels. They also enable vehicles to travel over soft ground, because they spread the load.

chassis The frame of a vehicle, including its wheels, suspension, and steering, but not the body or engine.

convoy A group of ships sailing together in formation for safety. They are protected by a screen of armed escort ships from attacks by submarines, aircraft, and surface warships.

corvette A small maneuverable escort ship widely used in World War II for convoy duties. Its top speed was a mere 16 knots.

crane A type of helicopter specially designed for lifting heavy loads of freight. These are slung beneath the fuselage.

D

D-Day The day chosen for the Allied invasion of north-west Europe (June 6, 1944). This assault was the largest sea-borne landing ever staged in war.

depth charge A high-explosive charge packed in a canister and set to explode when it reaches a given depth in the water. Depth charges are used to destroy submarines.

destroyer A small, fast, fighting ship. In World War II, destroyers were used to protect larger warships, and also formed the backbone of convoy escorts. They could steam at speeds up to 30–40 knots, and ranged widely in size. Their firepower included 5-inch guns, batteries of anti-aircraft guns, and torpedoes.

DUKW An American amphibious truck used for ferrying men and stores from large transport ships to beaches and onto dry land. The DUKW could travel on roads too.

E

escort carriers Small aircraft carriers often built on converted merchant hulls. They sometimes sailed with convoys to provide them with air cover over mid-ocean.

F

flanged wheel The wheels used to replace rubber tires when vehicles were converted to railways. They had an inner lip, or flange, to guide them along the tracks.

four-wheel drive The number of wheels that are directly powered by the engine determine the *drive* of a vehicle. Thus a vehicle that has four powered wheels is said to have four-wheel drive.

frigate The smallest type of destroyer used in World War II for such duties as escorting convoys was known by this name.

"funnies" A term often applied to specialized armored vehicles used by advancing formations. Often, they were built on tank chassis, and were employed to clear mines, bulldoze obstacles, bridge ditches, and provide cover for infantry.

G

gauge The width between the two rails of a railway is called the *gauge* of the track.

Goliath A miniature, remote-controlled tank used by the German forces to deliver high-explosive charges against enemy strongpoints.

H

half-tread A vehicle that has road wheels at the front for steering, and treads at the rear that drive it forward. Such machines have good cross-country performance.

hedgehog A throwing device that threw a pattern of 24 small charges ahead of a ship that was attacking a submarine.

H/F D/F Abbreviation for *High Frequency Direction Finder*, a device used to pinpoint the position of a submarine by homing in on its radio transmissions.

howitzer A powerful field gun with a short barrel that gives a high angle of fire. The plunging shells are useful for penetrating trenches and similarly protected positions. Howitzers were widely used in World War I to bombard front-line trenches.

I

infra-red sights Equipment that makes it possible for tank commanders to "see" in the dark. It makes night driving and firing possible.

J

jeep The original name of the famous small all-purpose truck used by the American armed forces was *GP*. This soon became changed to *jeep*. GP stands for *General Purpose* vehicle.

"Jimmy" The nickname for the standard 2½-ton truck used by the American forces in World War II.

K

knot A measure of speed by ships at sea, one knot (nautical mile per hour) equals 1.15 mph (1.85 kph). Thus, a ship steaming at 25 knots is traveling at about 29 mph (46 kph).

L

LCA Abbreviation for *Landing Craft Assault*. LCA's could carry up to 35 troops to an invasion beach from a transport ship lying offshore.

LCT Abbreviation for *Landing Craft Tank*. LCT's were larger types of landing craft able to carry up to five 40-ton tanks to an invasion beach.

Liberty ships Mass-produced American cargo ships that were turned out at great speed in World War II. More than 2,700 were built. Large numbers of new merchant ships were needed to replace those sunk by submarines and armed merchant cruisers.

limpet mine A mine that fastens to metal surfaces magnetically.

LST Abbreviation for *Landing Ship Tank*. LST's were large ships with a draft too deep to come close inshore. They were obliged to launch their cargoes some distance at sea, from where the amphibious tanks "swam" ashore under their own power.

M

Mark IV The most common tank of World War I. About 1,000 were built in the last two years of the war. The British Mark IV had two versions: the "male" had a six-pound gun, while the "female" was armed with heavy machine guns.

Maus The biggest tank ever built was the German *Maus* (Mouse), a 185-ton monster. It reached the experimental stage, but never went into full production.

Maxim gun An early, water-cooled machine gun used in World War I.

mechanized warfare This term describes the type of modern warfare that involves the use of vast numbers of machines for fighting and for transporting men and equipment.

merchantman A ship designed for carrying cargo. The various types of merchantmen include tankers, bulk carriers, and container ships.

mines High explosive charges buried

just beneath the surface on land, or lying on the bottom or floating at sea. Mines are designed to explode when an unwary person, vehicle, or ship passes over them.

mortar A weapon that lobs shells high in the air to hit enemies hidden behind hilltops or buildings, or in similar positions. Small mortars are used as infantry weapons. But some huge mortars have also been constructed to attack enemy strongpoints.

"Mulberries" Prefabricated concrete harbors that were towed in sections across the English Channel during the D-Day landing. They were reassembled off the beaches of Normandy to form "instant" harbors.

O

Oerlikon A 20-mm rapid-firing cannon often mounted on Allied ships in World War II.

P

Panzer The German term to describe armored fighting vehicles.

Panzerschrek An 88-mm recoilless anti-tank rocket launcher used by the German army in World War II. It worked on the same principle as a bazooka.

PIAT Projector Infantry Anti-Tank. An infantry anti-tank weapon used by British troops in World War II. It fired a projectile with a high-explosive warhead.

pom-pom A multi-barrel, quick-firing anti-aircraft gun.

Q

Q-ship A warship disguised as a merchantman that attacked merchant vessels belonging to enemy countries. Q-ships carried hidden guns. They would approach unsuspecting craft, and at the last moment open fire from close range.

R

radar An electronic device for detecting distant aircraft and ships by radio waves. Radar was widely used by ships in World War II to warn of approaching submarines and planes. An enemy vessel or plane would show up on the radar screen as a small illuminated blip. Radar was also useful for warning of the approach of ships and aircraft in the dark and in fog.

railroad bed The crushed gravel and rows of sleepers on which the rails are laid.

recoilless rifle A powerful rifle, often mounted on jeeps or armored vehicles and used to support raids.

reconnaissance The term for the patrol operations that sought information about enemy strength and positions and the general lie of the land.

re-supply ships Warships on station at sea often re-supplied themselves from tankers and storeships without having to return to their home bases. This technique was widely used by the German navy, which had little access to bases outside Europe.

rolling stock The cars pulled by a locomotive are referred to as *rolling stock*. They have no means of propulsion of their own.

S

sabotage Wartime sabotage usually involves acts of disruption by civilians against enemy troops occupying their country. Such acts include the blowing up of trains and bridges, and the destruction of military equipment. Sabotage can effectively pin down hundreds of enemy troops in guarding installations.

self-propelled gun A heavy gun mounted on a mobile chassis, and often armored to give the gun crew protection. It can drive itself from place to place on the battlefield, and does not need to be towed. Such guns are usually treaded to provide better cross-country performance.

sidecar The small "cart" that is sometimes attached to the side of a motorcycle to carry an extra passenger.

snorkel A simple tube-like device carried by submarines. It enabled them to breathe the air needed by their diesel engines while cruising underwater to avoid detection. Deep-wading tanks also used a snorkel device as they crawled along the bottom of rivers.

sonar An electronic system that transmits high-pitched sounds underwater and is used for detecting submarines. The sonar picks up the echoes of the sound as they are reflected back by the steel hull of a submarine. These echoes can be plotted so as to show the range and bearing of the ship.

squadron A small group of warships, often the same kind that sail together as a fighting unit.

superstructure That part of a ship that extends above the main deck and includes the guns, bridge, cabins, masts, and funnels.

T

tank A treaded, armored fighting vehicle. The name *tank* results from a British stratagem in World War I to conceal the existence of such vehicles. The new weapons were shipped to France in crates marked as water tanks for delivery to Russia. The name stuck for ever after.

tank crews Most modern tanks have an average crew of four or five men. This includes the driver, gunner, gunloader, and commander. But early tanks were such complicated machines that crews were far larger. The A7V, a monster German tank of World War I, was crewed by 18 men!

tank transporter The wear and tear of cross-country travel on the treads of a tank is enormous. When shipping tanks long distances, they are often loaded on trailers and pulled by tractor trucks.

torpedo An underwater weapon armed with an explosive warhead that goes off when the torpedo strikes its target. Torpedoes are self-propelled, and can be controlled for the direction and depth at which they are to run. Some torpedoes have a range of more than 15 miles (25 km).

trench warfare In World War I, both sides on the Western Front dug themselves into strong defensive positions. The war became static, with the opposing armies facing each other in long lines of trenches. The troops lived, fought, and died in trenches for almost all of the four-year conflict. When deep bunkers were built, even the heaviest shelling could do little to dislodge either side, or so weaken the line that an attack could burst through.

turret An enclosed and heavily armored mounting in which a large gun is housed. The turrets of tanks can swivel in all directions, allowing the main gun to fire at moving targets even while the tank itself is moving. On warships, turrets are the main gun emplacements.

U

U-boat The German name for submarine is *Unterseeboot*. This is commonly shortened to *U-boot* or *U-boat*.

W

waders Vehicles that are too heavy to float but can nevertheless move through water are known as *waders*. Deep waders, including some tanks, can travel underwater fully submerged.

Aircraft

How does a bird fly?

To fly like a bird! That dream inspired people for thousands of years. Story-tellers invented legends of people who flew on magic carpets, and others who tamed eagles and were carried on their backs. Some listeners believed these stories. Others knew that such things did not really happen. But they asked: "If the birds can fly, why cannot we, with our inventive brains, find a way of doing so?"

In Greek legend, Icarus flew with wings of wax. But the sun melted the wax, and he was killed.

A bird's wings are convex (curved outward) on their upper surfaces, and concave (curved inward) or flat underneath. As the bird flies, the air passing over its wings has to travel farther than that passing beneath. The result is a force that lifts the bird. But this force exists only while the bird is moving forward. To move forward, the bird flaps its wings. On the upstroke, the wing feathers part, and let the air through. On the downstroke, they come together and push the air down and back. To get into the air, the bird beats its wings downward and jumps at the same time.

Why did we take so long to understand flight?

People believed that the way to fly was to fix wings to their arms, and become "birds." But even if efficient wings could be made, no one would have the strength to use them. The bird is, proportionately, much stronger than we are. In the 1400's, the artist Leonardo da Vinci realized that some other means of flight was needed.

Leonardo designed an aer[ial] propeller to fly in much [the] same way as a mode[rn] helicopter does.

How does an airplane fly?

In flight, four forces act on an airplane: lift, gravity, thrust, and drag. Lift, the upward force, results from air moving across the wings when the airplane is traveling forward. The airplane stays in the air because the lift is strong enough to overcome the downward pull of gravity (the force that makes objects fall to Earth). The forward-driving thrust comes from a propeller, jet engine, or rocket motor.

Drag

Lift

Thrust

Gravity

1. Air has farther to go across the top of the wing. It travels faster. This creates lift. 2. At a steeper angle, lift is increased.

3. At too steep an angle, the air moves unevenly. Lift is lost, and the airplane stalls.

Wing Shape Creates Lift

1

2

3

Who were the first men to fly?

The first successful flights were achieved almost by accident. In the 1780's, two Frenchmen, Joseph-Michel and Jacques-Étienne Montgolfier, started to think about the fact that smoke from a fire always rises. It does so because hot air is lighter than cold. The Montgolfiers made balloons of cloth and paper, and lit small fires under them. The balloons filled with hot air—and flew!

When the Montgolfiers demonstrated a balloon, many people came to jeer. To their amazement, it soared into the sky.

A rooster, a duck and a lamb made a balloon flight. Then, in October, 1783, two men flew across Paris.

The first air letter in history was carried in a balloon in the United States in 1859.

The first international flight. In January, 1785, Jean-Pierre Blanchard and John Jeffries crossed the English Channel.

The first controlled flight was made in 1852 by the Frenchman Henri Giffard in his steam-driven airship.

What were the first airplanes like?

A real airplane! But it was only a toy. In 1804, Sir George Cayley fixed a kite to a piece of stick, added a small weight to keep the nose down, and threw his airplane—the first ever—into the air. To his delight, it sailed gracefully down a long hill. In the 1850's, using the same principle, he built a full-size glider. It is claimed that he persuaded his coachman to glide across a valley in it. Then, in 1874, a French naval officer, Félix du Temple, made a powered heavier-than-air machine. With a person on board, it actually rose into the air and made a hop of a few yards. Its engine probably operated on hot air.

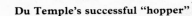

Cayley's model airplane

Du Temple's successful "hopper"

Cayley's glider

Who made the first real airplane flight?

Orville Wright

Wilbur Wright

THE GREAT BREAKTHROUGH On December 17, 1903, something happened that changed civilization. A gas-engined machine called Flyer I took off from the ground under its own power—and flew. It stayed in the air for 12 seconds, and covered a distance of about 120 feet (37 meters). At last somebody had made the great breakthrough that people had dreamed of for thousands of years.

The historic first flight was made by Orville Wright near the small settlement of Kitty Hawk, North Carolina. He and his brother Wilbur had invented and built *Flyer I*. They tossed a coin to decide who should be the first to pilot it. Later in the day, Wilbur made a flight of some 853 feet (260 meters) and stayed in the air for 59 seconds.

Kitty Hawk

What was the plane like?

Flyer I had wings more than 40 feet (12 meters) long. They were made of wooden frames covered with cotton. The 12-horsepower engine had four cylinders.

Fabric-covered wings

Propellers rotate in opposite directions. They "push" the plane.

Wooden ribs and struts

Liquid-cooled 12-hp engine

Elevators at front

Flyer I

The plane flew "tail first." The pilot lay on his stomach in the center of the lower wing, with the engine beside him.

Twin steering-rudders at rear

Wires operating wing-warping

Elevator control

A Rival

Another American, Samuel P. Langley, had earlier built a successful model plane. He called it an *Aerodrome*. On December 7 and 8, 1903, he tried to catapult a full-scale *Aerodrome* into the air. But on each occasion it caught in the launching gear.

Aerodrome

Did Flyer I have controls?

Twin rudders steered the plane in flight.

Elevators were used for climbing and diving.

The wing tips were warped (twisted) by wires to bank the plane when turning.

The pilot moved his body in a "cradle" to twist the wing tips. He controlled the elevators with a lever.

Control Levers

The Propeller

A propeller provides thrust by "screwing" its way through the air.

The Wrights thought of the propeller as a moving wing.

What were other pioneer planes like?

Wright Flyer III (1905). It could stay in the air for 30 minutes, and could bank, turn, and circle.

Alberto Santos-Dumont's 14-bis (1906). It made the first official flight in Europe—about 200 feet (60 meters).

Santos-Dumont's Demoiselle (1909). It could fly at nearly 60 mph (100 kph).

Voisin-Farman (1908). In it Henry Farman flew a 1-kilometer circle in 1 minute 28 seconds, at Issy-les-Moulineaux, in France.

Glenn H. Curtiss's June Bug (1903). It flew about 1,280 feet (390 meters).

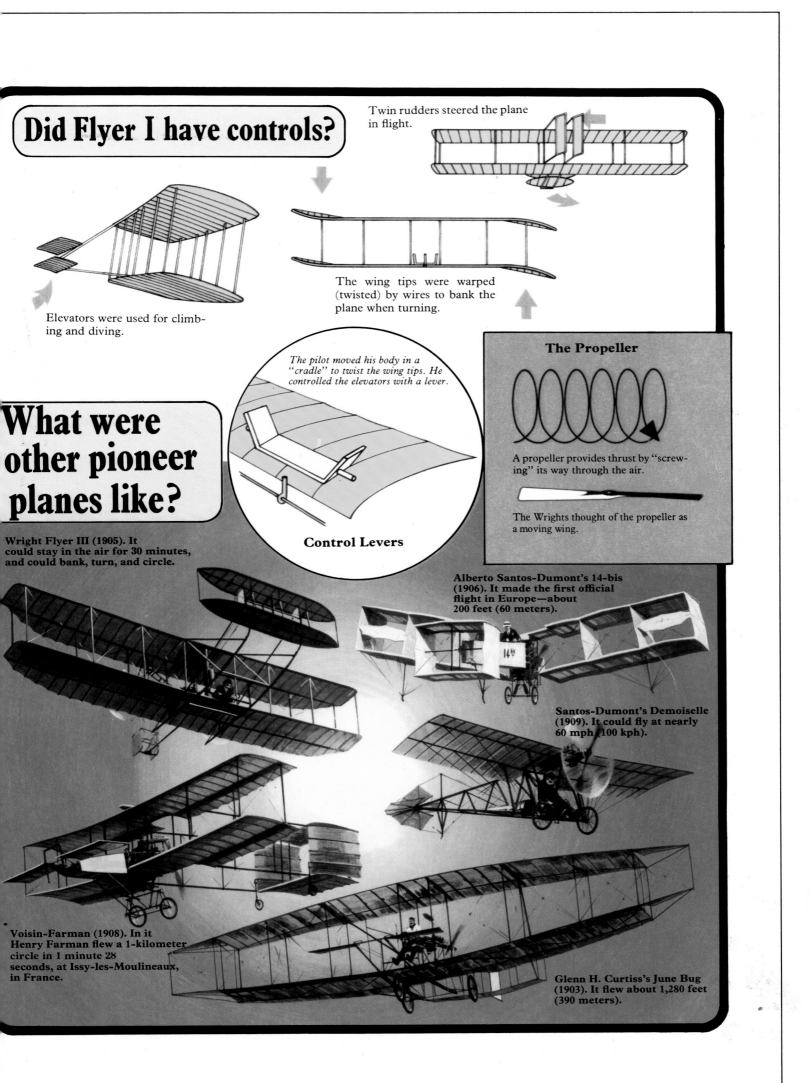

THE AIRPLANE GROWS UP The Wright brothers' success proved that controlled flight was possible. Other pioneers were spurred on to even greater efforts. Within years, many reliable flying machines had been built. The airplane's development was encouraged by prizes for speed or other evidence of progress.

Why did the pioneers build planes with so many wings?

Avro Triplane (1909)

Sikorsky, Le Grand (1913)

A famous monoplane: Douglas DC-3 (1935)

Many of the slow early airplanes had two or more sets of wings, so that the large wing area would give maximum lift. As planes grew more powerful and faster, the monoplane became supreme.

Fokker Dr-1 (1917)

Can airplanes land on water?

Canadair CL-215 (1969)

Cessna Super Skywagon

SEAPLANE

FLYING BOAT

Two main kinds of airplanes operate from water instead of land—seaplanes and flying boats. Seaplanes (also called floatplanes) have floats in place of landing wheels. Flying boats have boat-like fuselages (bodies).

Air Speed Records

	mph	kph
1909 Wright biplane	34.04	54.77
1909 Curtiss biplane	43.35	69.75
1910 Blériot monoplane	68.18	109.73
1913 Deperdussin	126.64	203.81
1920 Nieuport-Delage 29	194.50	313.00
1923 Curtiss R-2 C-1	267.16	429.96
1928 Macchi M-52bis	318.57	512.69
1931 Supermarine S.6B	406.94	654.90
1934 Macchi M.C.72	440.56	709.07
1939 Messerschmitt Me 209 V-1	469.12	754.97
1946 Gloster Meteor F4	615.65	990.79
1947 Lockheed P-80R	623.61	1,003.60
1953 North American YF-100A	755.00	1,215.04
1955 North American F-100C	822.10	1,323.03
1956 Fairey Delta 2	1,132.00	1,821.39
1958 Lockheed F-104A Starfighter	1,403.80	2,259.18
1961 McDonnell F4H-1F Phantom 2	1,606.51	2,585.43
1965 Lockheed YF-12A	2,070.10	3,331.51
1976 Lockheed SR-71A	2,193.17	3,529.56

What was the Schneider Trophy?

The Schneider Trophy was presented by a French manufacturer, Jacques Schneider, in 1913 to encourage the development of seaplanes and flying boats. It was awarded to the winner of a yearly race. The Trophy was won outright by Britain in 1931 for three victories—in 1927, 1929, and 1931.

Supermarine S.6B

The Supermarine S.6B won the Schneider Trophy in 1931.

Macchi M.C.72

The S.6B and the M.C.72 both broke world air speed records.

How big were the first airliners?

← 89 feet 9 inches (27.36 meters) →

Handley Page HP 42 (1930). Known for comfort and reliability, the HP 42 operated mainly on European routes.

← 231 feet 4 inches (70.49 meters) →

Boeing 747 (1970). The first of the jumbo jets, the Boeing 747 has passenger lounges on two "stories."

The early airliners were considered marvels of speed, comfort, and safety. They made flying a normal way of traveling. But compared with today's airliners, they were small and slow.

What are the main controls?

Elevator

Rudde[r]

Elevat[or]

Aileron

Control column

Rudder pedals

Aileron

WHAT THE PILOT DOES The principles of flight are the same for a modern jet airliner as they were for the first "string and cardboard" planes. But over the years, the airplane has developed into one of the most complex pieces of machinery in existence. As a result, airline pilots of today are faced with hundreds of controls and instruments. Each is necessary for aircraft to be operated safely.

In their simplest form, the main controls are foot pedals to operate the rudder, and a control column to operate elevators and ailerons. The column is moved forward or back to control the elevators, left or right to control the ailerons.

How does a pilot take off?

As soon as the control tower gives a pilot clearance for take-off, he taxies to the runway. He heads the plane into the wind, with the engines at full power. He keeps the control column forward until the plane has enough speed. Then he eases it back, to hinge the elevators upward. The plane's nose lifts, and the aircraft begins to climb. At the desired height, he puts the column to neutral to level off.

Control column forward

Control column back

Control column neutral

How does a pilot turn?

To turn the plane in flight, the pilot uses both the rudder pedals and the control column. To make a left turn, he pushes the left pedal. The rudder swings left, and the airflow pushes the tail to the right. At the same time, the pilot moves the column to the left: the left aileron hinges up, and the right aileron down. The plane then banks (leans) left into the turn, as a bicycle does on a corner.

Left pedal forward

Right pedal forward

Rudder swings left

Rudder swings right

Plane turns left

Plane turns right

How does a pilot land?

The plane descends with the column forward and the elevators hinged downward. The pilot reduces speed, and levels the plane off. At touch-down, he eases the column back, then pushes it to neutral.

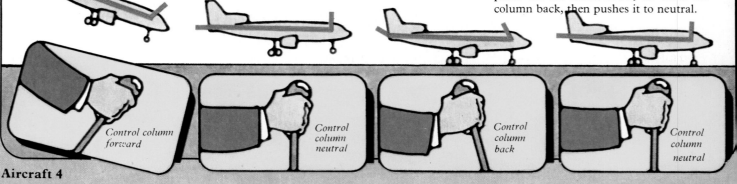

Control column forward

Control column neutral

Control column back

Control column neutral

What does the pilot see?

In the flight deck of an airliner, the captain and the co-pilot sit before a vast display of dials, levers, and switches. The captain sits in the left-hand seat. The chief instruments before each of the pilots are arranged in the "basic T." They show the airspeed, the aircraft's "attitude," the altitude, and the course. Other instruments indicate the performance of the engine and the various other systems of the airliner—for example, the fuel supply and the landing gear. For much of the flight, the plane may "fly itself" on automatic pilot.

Airspeed Indicator, *top left,* shows the pilot how fast he is flying.

Attitude Indicator, *center top,* shows the plane's attitude in relation to an artificial horizon. It enables the pilot to fly straight and level, and to make accurate changes of direction.

Altimeter, *above,* shows the pilot the altitude (height above sea level) at which he is flying.

Course Indicator, *left,* a radio compass, enables the pilot to follow the exact course—path through the sky—that he wishes.

What are the main sections of an airport?

Runways

Taxiways

Fuel store

Aircraft maintenance hangars

Car parks

Passenger boarding gates

Main terminal control tower

Passenger terminal, with lounges, shops, and restaurants

Cargo terminal

THE AIRPORT A large airport is a very busy place. Each day, thousands of passengers pass through it and hundreds of airliners use its runways. It has a large permanent "population" too—traffic controllers, weather bureau staff, mechanics, police, firemen, doctors, airline personnel, and many others.

Why is the control tower important?

The control tower is the airport's nerve center. It controls all aircraft on the ground, as well as those approaching or leaving the runways.

Aircraft 5

How does a busy airport avoid aerial collisions?

An airplane approaching an airport is directed by ground control to join a "stack" of waiting aircraft. The planes circle at strictly controlled distances.

By means of radio beams, ground control can guide a plane to a safe landing. A localizer beam tells the pilot when he is in line with the center of the runway. A glide path beam gives him the correct angle of descent. The pilot can read this information on his instruments.

How is an airliner brought in to land?

Plane leaves stack, and prepares to land

Localizer beam lines plane up with center of runway

Runway

INSTRUMENT LANDING SYSTEM (ILS)

Radio marker beacons tell pilot his distance from runway

Glide path beam marks correct glide path to beginning of runway

What happens after it lands?

On stand-by: vehicles and crews of the fire and crash service

Hydraulic loading platform

British airways

Refuelling tanker

Water tanker

Catering vehicle delivering food and drink

Mobile stairs

Tug for moving aircraft when engines not running

After the plane touches down, the control tower directs it to an unloading ramp. The pilot checks the instruments, and completes the record of the flight in the logbook. The passengers leave the plane, and their baggage is unloaded.

The pilot reports the completion of his flight plan.

The baggage is unloaded, and sent to the arrival lounge.

The plane is checked by engineers, and refuelled for its next flight.

Passenger and crew compartments of the plane are cleaned.

Fire-fighting services stand by, ready for emergencies.

Food and drink are loaded, ready for serving to passengers in flight.

What is the difference between a helicopter and an airplane?

An airplane has fixed wings as well as a means of propulsion (forward movement) such as an engine-driven propeller or a jet engine. A helicopter has a rotor (a set of thin blade-like wings) on top that spins around and acts both as wings and propeller. Another smaller rotor at the back holds it steady.

Rudder controls turning movement

AIRPLANE

Wing provides lift   *Propeller provides thrust*

Main rotor provides lift and thrust

Tail rotor controls turning movement

HELICOPTER

How is a helicopter controlled?

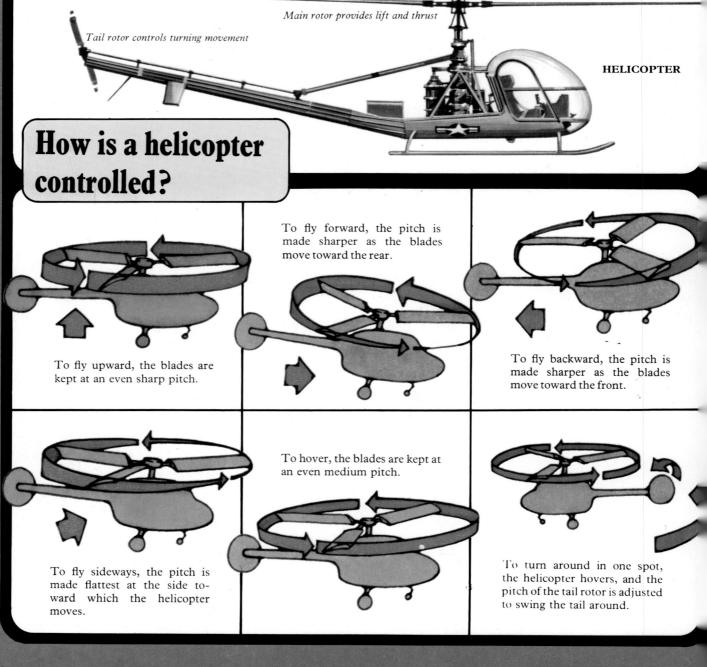

To fly upward, the blades are kept at an even sharp pitch.

To fly forward, the pitch is made sharper as the blades move toward the rear.

To fly backward, the pitch is made sharper as the blades move toward the front.

To fly sideways, the pitch is made flattest at the side toward which the helicopter moves.

To hover, the blades are kept at an even medium pitch.

To turn around in one spot, the helicopter hovers, and the pitch of the tail rotor is adjusted to swing the tail around.

Who invented the helicopter?

The idea of the helicopter dates back hundreds of years. Leonardo da Vinci drew a suggested helicopter in about 1500. In 1784, two Frenchmen named Launoy and Bienvenu made a model helicopter that flew. Another Frenchman, Paul Cornu, invented a machine that lifted a man off the ground in 1907. Other forerunners of the modern helicopter were Étienne Oemichen's machine of 1922 and Juan de la Cierva's autogiro of 1923.

Oemichen No. 2

Leonardo's design

Launoy and Bienvenu's model

Cornu's helicopter

La Cierva autogiro

What are helicopters used for?

Police patrol

Air taxi

Air-sea rescue

The adaptable helicopter is used by police and by fire and rescue services. Farmers use it for crop spraying. It serves as a taxi, and as a crane for lifting loads in places where no ordinary crane could go.

What is the difference between an airship and a balloon?

THE FLYING GIANTS Airships are the largest machines that fly. They stay in the air because they are filled with lighter-than-air gases—hydrogen or helium. Hydrogen is lighter than helium, but is dangerous because it is highly inflammable. Several famous airships that used it were destroyed by fire. To many people, the airship is the most romantic of all aircraft.

BALLOON

Elevator

Engines

Rudder

NON-RIGID AIR

Both balloons and airships stay in the air because they are filled with a light gas. But a balloon is free-flying: it travels where the wind carries it. An airship has engines to carry it forward, and elevators and a rudder to control its direction of flight.

How is an airship built?

Airships may be non-rigid or rigid. In a non-rigid airship, or *blimp*, the gas is contained in a simple, streamlined bag called the *envelope*. In a rigid airship, the envelope is supported by an inside metal framework.

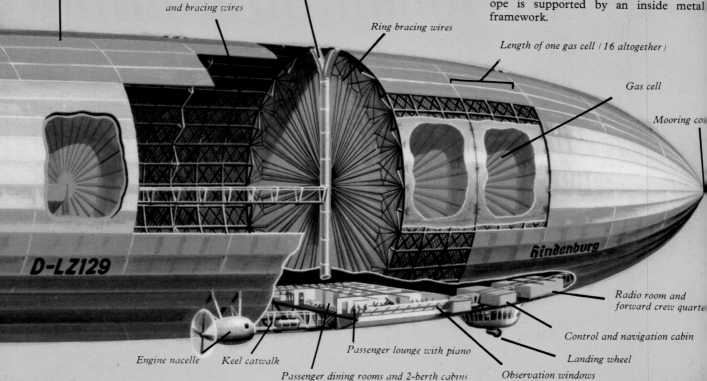

Doped fabric outer envelope

Framework of lightweight girders and bracing wires

Gas and ventilation shaft

Ring bracing wires

Length of one gas cell (16 altogether)

Gas cell

Mooring co

D-LZ129

Hindenburg

Engine nacelle　*Keel catwalk*

Passenger lounge with piano

Passenger dining rooms and 2-berth cabins

Radio room and forward crew quarte

Control and navigation cabin

Landing wheel

Observation windows

How big are airships?

The great passenger airships, the giants in the sky, were almost as long as ocean-going liners. The German airship *Hindenburg* was nearly 804 feet (245 meters) long—the length of about 30 buses. The fastest airships could fly at more than 75 mph (120 kph).

What is it like to fly in one?

Passenger airships had sleeping cabins, lounges, and dining rooms where passengers sat at tables. The lounge of the *Hindenburg* even contained a piano—though one made of aluminum.

Famous Airships

Deutschland (1910), one of the first passenger Zeppelins. The German Zeppelin airships were named after Count Ferdinand von Zeppelin, inventor of the rigid airship.

R 101 (British; 1929)

LZ 129 Hindenburg (German; 1936)

Macon (American; 1933), with its "hook-on" Curtiss F9C Sparrowhawk fighter airplanes.

Are they still used today?

Goodyear airship at night. Its computer-controlled advertising lights display "moving" pictures.

U.S. Navy Type ZPG-2

Today, airships are curiosities. A few small airships are still seen in the skies. They are used for advertising. The United States Navy had some airships until the 1960's, and flew them as part of a radar early-warning system.

How does a jet engine work?

THE JET AGE   The principle of the jet engine is simple, and has been known for a long time. But a practical jet engine was not invented until about 1930, and the first jet airplane did not fly until 1939. Since then, the jet engine has made the piston-driven propeller a thing of the past, except for the smallest planes. The jet has caused a revolution in aviation. Today, airplanes with jet engines fly at speeds that the early pioneers would not have believed possible.

Inside pressures are equal

Balloon moves by reaction to backward jet of air

Combustion chamber: fuel and compressed air burn

Compressor sucks in air

Turbine spins compressor

Exhaust nozzle

A toy balloon demonstrates the jet principle. While the neck is held closed, inside pressures are equal in all directions, and the balloon does not try to move. But when the neck is released, the balloon flies away. Reaction to the air shooting out of the neck drives it forward.

How many kinds of jet engines are there?

In a jet engine, air is sucked in, and a compressor pumps it under pressure into a combustion chamber. There, it is mixed with fuel, and burned. The resulting gases rush at high speed out of the exhaust nozzle. As with the balloon, reaction drives the engine (and the airplane) forward.

Turbojet: Air is sucked in, compressed, and burned, forming a jet of hot gases.

Turbofan: Some compressed air bypasses the combustion chamber.

Turboprop: The hot gases form a jet, and also drive a propeller.

Ram-jet: Forward movement "rams" air into the combustion chamber. No compressor.

What were the first jet planes?

Heinkel He 178

Caproni-Campini N.1

Gloster E.28/29

Bell XP–59A Airacomet

The jet age began on August 27, 1939, when the little He 178 monoplane designed by the German engineer Ernst Heinkel made its first flight. It reached a speed of 435 mph (700 kph). The plane's turbojet engine was designed by Pabst von Ohain. Earlier, Heinkel had made a successful rocket-plane, the He 176. In August, 1940, a piston-engined jet took to the air in Italy. It was called the Caproni-Campini N.1, after its engine-designer Secondo Campini and its constructors Caproni. It flew at about 130 mph (210 kph). In Britain, a jet research airplane, the Gloster E.28/29, flew successfully in May, 1941. It was powered by a turbojet designed by Frank Whittle. An American jet airplane flew in October, 1942. It was called the Bell XP-59A *Airacomet*, and had two turbojet engines based on Frank Whittle's engine.

Are rockets jets?

A rocket moves through the air by burning a fuel that gives off a jet of exhaust gases. It differs from other jet engines, because it does not need oxygen from the air to burn its fuel. It carries its own oxygen in a liquid called an *oxidizer*. Rockets can travel in space—in regions where there is no air and other types of jet engine would not work.

LIQUID-FUEL ROCKET

Oxidizer

Fuel

Pumps

Combustion chamber

How fast does sound travel?

SUPERSONIC FLIGHT Until the 1940's, the only artificial objects that had traveled faster than sound were bullets and artillery shells. But airplane speeds had greatly increased, and some could now approach the speed of sound. Pilots found that, at that speed, their planes seemed to fly into an invisible "barrier" through which they had to fight their way.

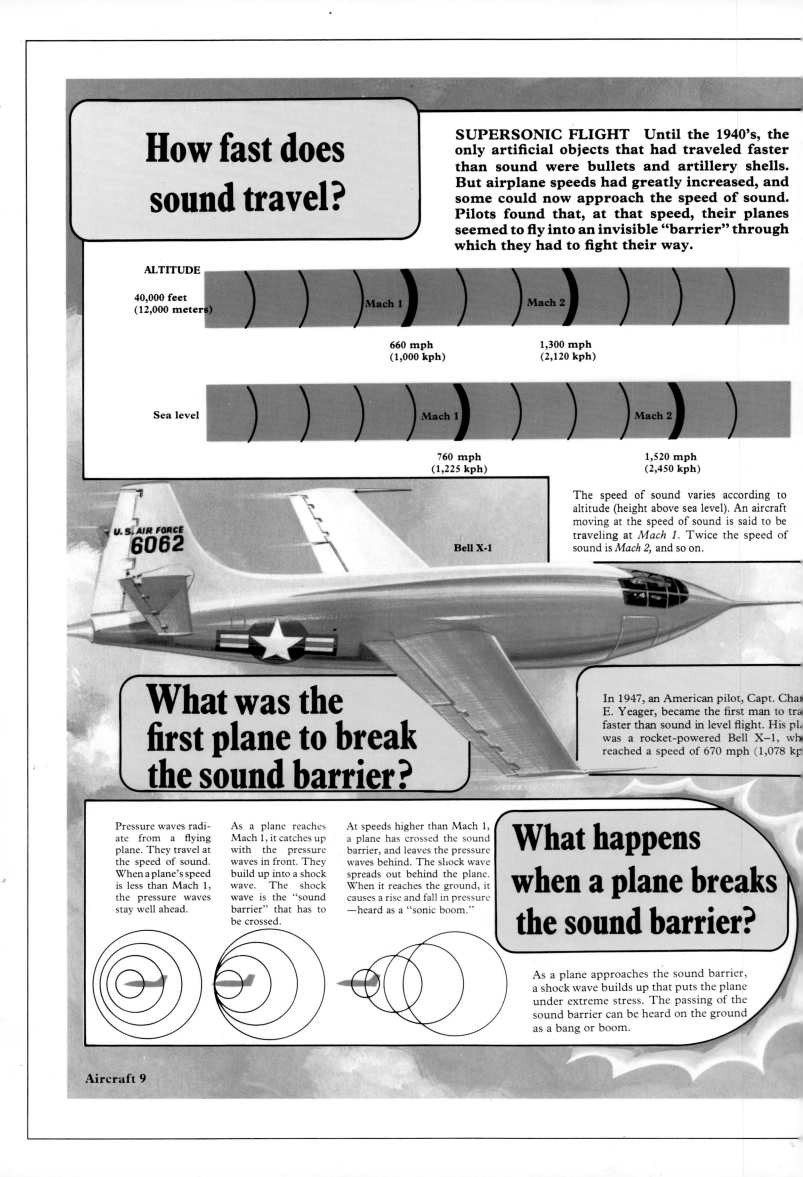

ALTITUDE

40,000 feet (12,000 meters)

Mach 1

Mach 2

660 mph (1,000 kph)

1,300 mph (2,120 kph)

Sea level

Mach 1

Mach 2

760 mph (1,225 kph)

1,520 mph (2,450 kph)

The speed of sound varies according to altitude (height above sea level). An aircraft moving at the speed of sound is said to be traveling at *Mach 1*. Twice the speed of sound is *Mach 2*, and so on.

U.S. AIR FORCE 6062

Bell X-1

What was the first plane to break the sound barrier?

In 1947, an American pilot, Capt. Cha[rles] E. Yeager, became the first man to tra[vel] faster than sound in level flight. His pl[ane] was a rocket-powered Bell X–1, wh[ich] reached a speed of 670 mph (1,078 kp[h]

Pressure waves radiate from a flying plane. They travel at the speed of sound. When a plane's speed is less than Mach 1, the pressure waves stay well ahead.

As a plane reaches Mach 1, it catches up with the pressure waves in front. They build up into a shock wave. The shock wave is the "sound barrier" that has to be crossed.

At speeds higher than Mach 1, a plane has crossed the sound barrier, and leaves the pressure waves behind. The shock wave spreads out behind the plane. When it reaches the ground, it causes a rise and fall in pressure —heard as a "sonic boom."

What happens when a plane breaks the sound barrier?

As a plane approaches the sound barrier, a shock wave builds up that puts the plane under extreme stress. The passing of the sound barrier can be heard on the ground as a bang or boom.

Is there a limit to the speed airplanes can travel?

At high supersonic speeds, heat and the finding of a suitable fuel become problems. There may be other problems yet unknown. Whether "spacecraft speeds" are possible for aircraft remains to be seen.

North American X-15 rocket-powered research aircraft. It reached a speed of 4,534 mph (7,297 kph) in 1967.

Lockheed SR-71A reconnaissance aircraft. It gained the official air speed record in 1976 with a speed of 2,193 mph (3,529 kph).

The Wright brothers' Flyer I made the first successful airplane flight in December, 1903. It flew at about 7 mph (11 kph).

In the less than 80 years since the Wright brothers' first slow, shaky little flight, the airplane has become able to fly at many times the speed of sound. The next 80 years may see equally amazing changes.

PLANES OF TODAY The technical problems of flight have long been mastered. But airplane designers still search for something better—planes that are bigger, or faster, or easier to handle, or cheaper to operate.

How big are the jumbo jets?

Boeing 747, the first commercial jumbo jet. It is 231 feet (70.4 meters) long.

Lockheed C-5A Galaxy. It can carry nearly 120 tons of cargo, and has 28 landi wheels.

The search for economy has led to the introduction of enormous "jumbo" planes. Though small compared with airships, they are the largest heavier-than-air craft.

Aero Spacelines Guppy, a propeller-driven giant built to carry unusually bulky loads. It is nearly 144 feet (44 meters) long.

Breguet 14T2

What are the fastest airliners?

Concorde

The Anglo-French *Concorde* and the Russian Tu-144 airliners can travel at supersonic speeds. But because of their noise, many people object to such planes flying over populated areas.

Tu-144

The Breguet 14T2 airliner operated on the London to Paris route in 1919. It carried two or three passengers, and flew at about 120 mph (190 kph). Though tiny by the standards of today, it was, in its time, considered a large airplane. The Boeing 747, which went into service in 1970, can carry up to 490 passengers, and has an upstairs lounge. It flies at around 600 mph (970 kph).

Why do some supersonic planes have swing wings?

Wings swept back for high-speed flight.

Grumman F-14A Tomcat

Wings extended for take-off, low-speed flight, and landing.

Wing can be swept back

For take-off, low-speed flight, and landing, the "bird wing" type of wing—almost at right angles to the fuselage—gives maximum lift. But the swept-back delta wing offers less drag at high speeds. The swing wing (or variable geometry) airplane can change its wing shape in flight according to speed.

What is a jump jet?

Hawker Siddeley T2 Harrier (1960)

Rolls Royce TMR Flying Bedstead (1953)

Lockheed XFV-1 (1954)

As airplanes have become faster and bigger, they have needed longer runways for taking off and landing. The jump jet or VTOL (vertical take-off and landing) airplane is designed to rise vertically into the air—as a helicopter does—and then fly as an ordinary plane.

How does a glider stay in the air?

DRAG

LIFT

THRUST

GRAVITY

602

GLIDERS AND GLIDING A glider sails through the air gracefully, like a seagull. It has no engine, and its flight is silent. But in the right weather conditions it can perform many of the same maneuvers as a powered airplane. And it can fly at speeds of up to about 95 miles an hour (150 kilometers an hour). Most gliders are flown for sport. Gliding clubs hold local competitions, and there are national and international championships.

A glider flies in the same way as a powered airplane. But because it has no engine, it has to get its forward thrust by gliding slowly "downhill" through the air. Its long wings help to give the maximum amount of lift. And it is streamlined so that there is little drag.

How can it climb and soar?

Cumulus clouds

Glider spirals upward

As well as gliding "downhill," a glider pilot can soar (gain height) by using *thermals*—rising currents of warm air. He flies around and around within a thermal, spiraling upward as the air rises. By moving from one thermal to another, he can sometimes fly his glider very long distances.

Warm air rising

Glider flies back and forth along ridge

Does the pilot depend on thermals for soaring?

Wind rises over hill or ridge

When wind blows against a hill or ridge, it is forced upward. A glider pilot can take advantage of this rising air to gain height. And he can stay aloft for long periods by flying back and forth along the hill or ridge in a figure-eight pattern.

How does a glider get into the air?

Launch by a powered aircraft

Launch by a motor vehicle

Launch by a winch

Launch from a cliff

Once a glider is airborne, it can stay aloft. But it cannot get into the air under its own power. It needs to be launched. This can be done in several ways. The glider may be towed into the air by a powered aircraft. Or it can be pulled into the sky like a kite, by a motor vehicle or a winch. Gliders are also launched by being cata-pulted from cliffs or hilltops. Some gliders have small engines used solely for taking off.

In war, gliders can be used to carry troops and equipment into places not easily reached by other means. Often, glider-borne troops operate together with parachute troops.

Are gliders used in war?

Who first used aircraft in war?

THE AIRPLANE BECOMES A WEAPON The pioneers of aviation saw only the peaceful uses of the airplane. They thought of flying as a sport, as a means of speeding up communications, and as a way of bringing the peoples of the world closer together. But in war, aircraft became deadly weapons—among the most destructive ever invented.

Balloons were the first aircraft used in war. *Above:* Unmanned Austrian balloons bomb Venice in 1849. *Left:* The German siege of Paris, 1870–71. Balloons leave the surrounded city at night, carrying passengers and mail.

How were they used in World War I?

At the beginning of World War I, most generals thought that airplanes had little use in battle. Occasionally, planes were sent up to act as aerial observation posts or as "eyes in the sky"—finding out what was happening behind enemy lines. But gradually, military planners realized the airplane's offensive power. Small planes from opposing sides fought battles in the air. Large bombing aircraft carried the war into enemy territory. *Left:* A British B.E.2a directs artillery fire onto an enemy column.

What were the first bombers like?

Several of the warring nations built long-range bombing planes. The Germans at first used Zeppelin airships to bomb England. But, unlike airplanes, these were easily shot down.

Zeppelin L.Z.8 Deutschland II

Handley Page 0/400 bomber

Caproni Ca 42 bomber

What was a "dog fight"?

Like knights of old, the fighter pilots of the opposing countries fought one-to-one battles. They had no support from the ground, and each pilot relied mainly on his own courage and skill. Pilots who gained a large number of victories in these aerial "dog fights" became famous as "aces."

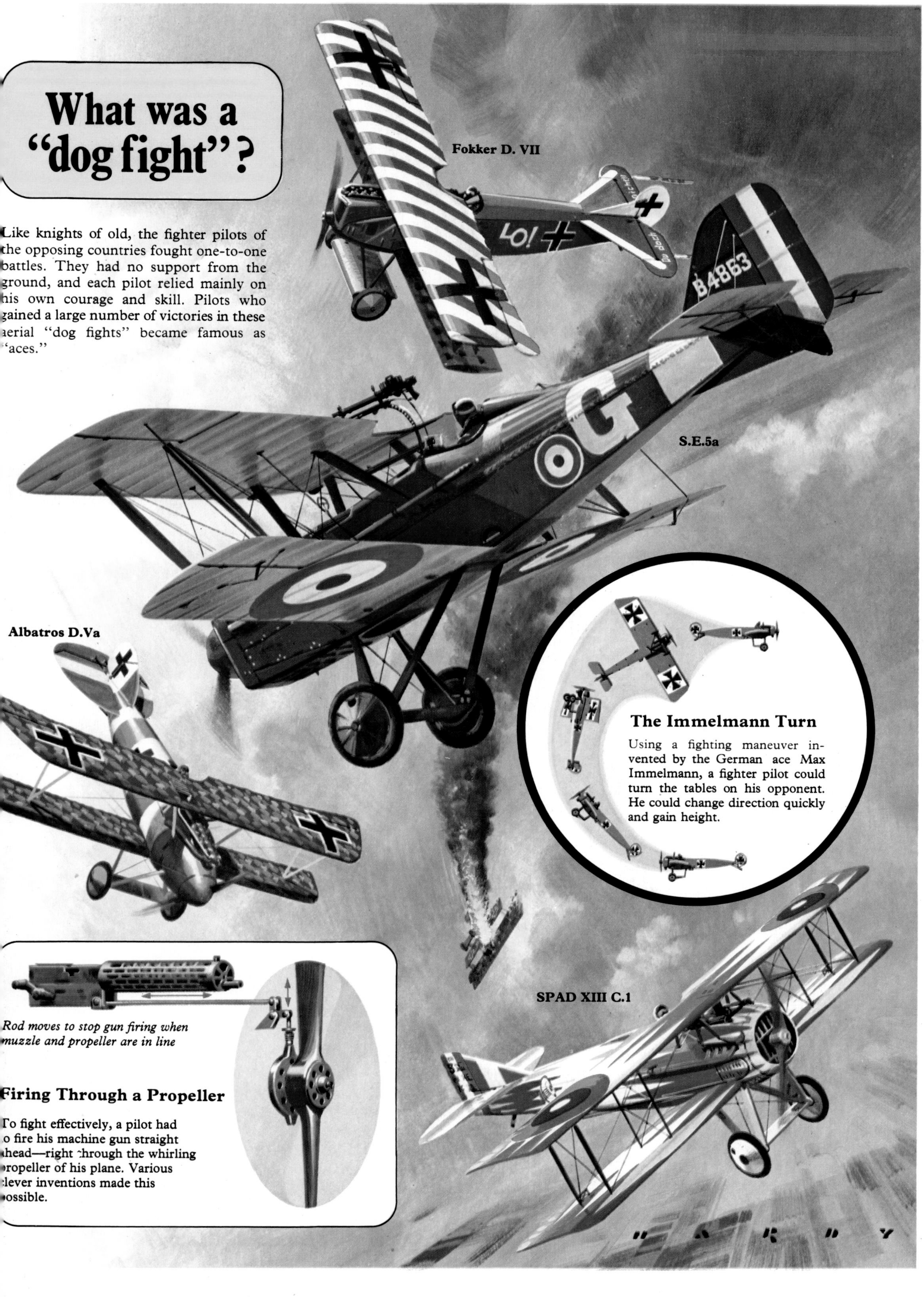

Fokker D. VII

S.E.5a

Albatros D.Va

The Immelmann Turn

Using a fighting maneuver invented by the German ace Max Immelmann, a fighter pilot could turn the tables on his opponent. He could change direction quickly and gain height.

Rod moves to stop gun firing when muzzle and propeller are in line

Firing Through a Propeller

To fight effectively, a pilot had to fire his machine gun straight ahead—right through the whirling propeller of his plane. Various clever inventions made this possible.

SPAD XIII C.1

Supermarine Spitfire

AIRCRAFT IN WORLD WAR II The airplane played only a small part in World War I. The war's great battles were fought by armies and navies. But in World War II, air forces became at least as important as any of the other fighting services. Several battles that were turning points in the war were fought in the air. And huge fleets of bombers attacked enemy cities and communications.

Bristol Beaufighter Mk. X

Famous fighter planes

Messerschmitt Bf-109

Republic P-47 Thunderbolt

The fighter aircraft of World War II no longer took part in "dog fights." They were now the fastest and most advanced planes in the world. Their chief tasks were to destroy enemy bombers, and protect the bombers of their own side. By the end of the war, they were armed with cannons and rockets, and were aided by radar.

Focke-Wulf Fw-190

North American P-51 Mustang

The terrifying dive bomber

One of the most frightening planes of the war was the dive bomber. It was a light plane, carrying only a few bombs. Instead of aiming its bombs from a height, it dived at its target with an ear-splitting shriek. At the last moment, it released its bombs, and climbed away. Sometimes, sirens on its wings increased its noise.

Fiat G-55 Centauro

Mitsubishi A6M3 Zero

Dewoitine D-520

Junkers Ju-87 Stuka

Slow but deadly: the bombers

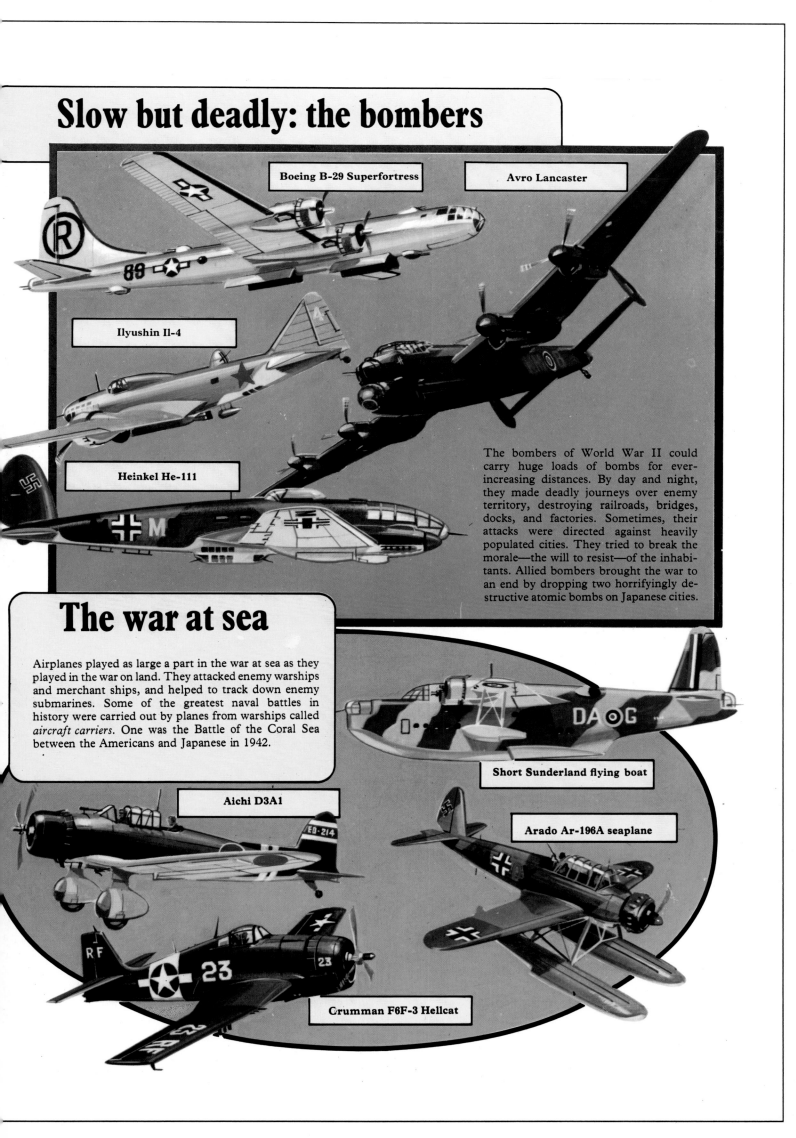

Boeing B-29 Superfortress

Avro Lancaster

Ilyushin Il-4

Heinkel He-111

The bombers of World War II could carry huge loads of bombs for ever-increasing distances. By day and night, they made deadly journeys over enemy territory, destroying railroads, bridges, docks, and factories. Sometimes, their attacks were directed against heavily populated cities. They tried to break the morale—the will to resist—of the inhabitants. Allied bombers brought the war to an end by dropping two horrifyingly destructive atomic bombs on Japanese cities.

The war at sea

Airplanes played as large a part in the war at sea as they played in the war on land. They attacked enemy warships and merchant ships, and helped to track down enemy submarines. Some of the greatest naval battles in history were carried out by planes from warships called *aircraft carriers*. One was the Battle of the Coral Sea between the Americans and Japanese in 1942.

Short Sunderland flying boat

Aichi D3A1

Arado Ar-196A seaplane

Grumman F6F-3 Hellcat

Strange airplanes

Clement Ader's steam-powered Éole (1890) managed to "hop" about 160 feet (50 meters).

The giant Ca-60 flying boat (1921) had nine sets of wings. It made only two flig[...]

The Grade aerobatic monoplane (1913) could fly and land upside-down.

Many strange airplanes have appeared in the skies. Some, such as the Caproni Ca-60 and the Rotabuggy, were not-very-successful attempts to solve problems. Others, including the Gee Bee Super Sportster, were designed for a purpose and had considerable success. Some, such as the Bell X-22A and the Ryan Flex-wing, were experimental. A few—for example, the Grade monoplane—were built for fun. But many of the strangest planes never lifted themselves into the skies at all. The Éole is one that made a valiant effort to do so.

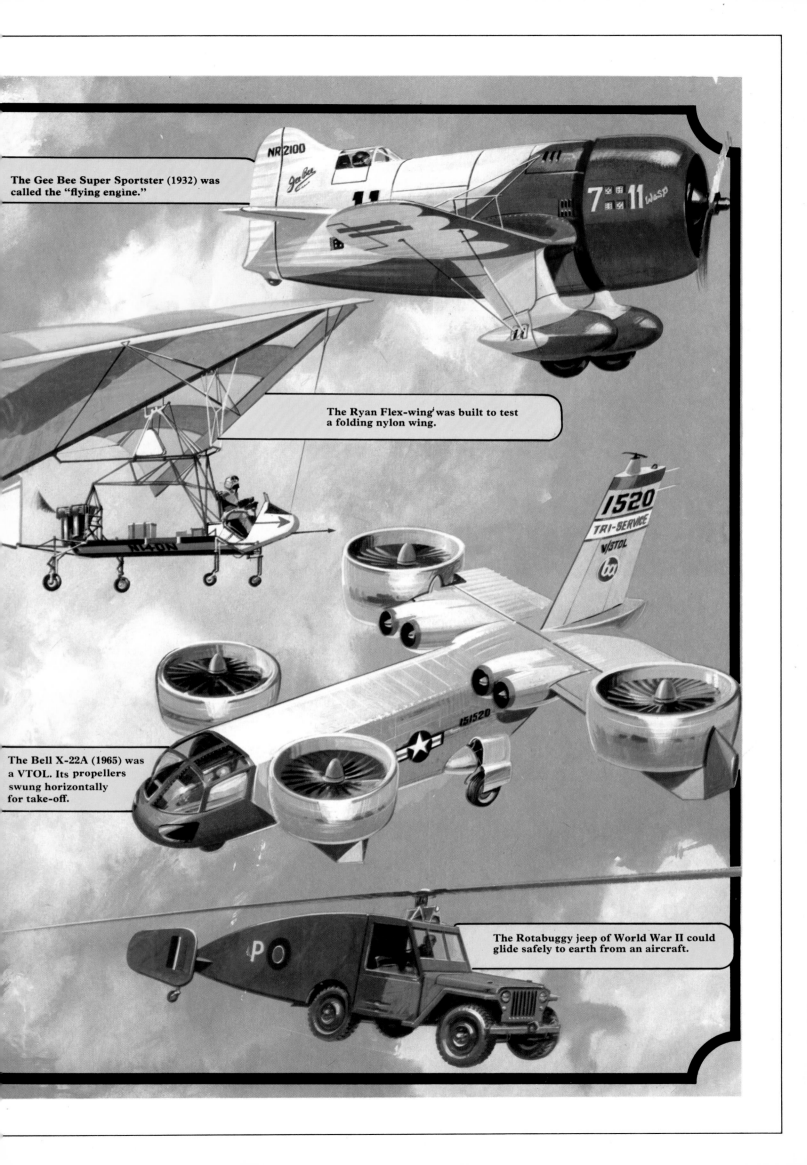

The Gee Bee Super Sportster (1932) was called the "flying engine."

The Ryan Flex-wing was built to test a folding nylon wing.

The Bell X-22A (1965) was a VTOL. Its propellers swung horizontally for take-off.

The Rotabuggy jeep of World War II could glide safely to earth from an aircraft.

A-Z of Aircraft

A

advanced technology engine Modern jet engine in which the turbines revolve at different speeds, resulting in low noise and better performance.

aerobatics "Aerial acrobatics" by aircraft as fighting maneuvers, or for testing, training, or entertainment.

aerodynamics The study of air movement around an object—usually air movement around an aircraft.

aeronautics The science or art of flight by aircraft.

aerospace The region around the Earth in which machines can fly.

aerostat A balloon or an airship—a lighter-than-air craft.

aileron A flap on the trailing edge of a wing, controlling an aircraft's rolling or banking movements.

airbus A large, short-range airliner.

aircraft A flying machine—usually an airplane.

aircraft carrier A warship designed to carry aircraft and act as a floating airdrome.

airdrome An airfield or airport. Today, the term usually refers to a small airport.

airfoil A surface designed to produce lift—such as an airplane wing.

airframe The body of an aircraft, minus the engine and controls.

airliner A transport aircraft used for carrying passengers and operated by an airline company.

airplane A flying machine with fixed wings and a means of forward thrust, such as an engine.

air pocket Wind disturbance causing an aircraft to bounce.

airship A lighter-than-air flying machine, differing from a balloon because it has an engine (or engines) and controls.

airspeed The speed of an aircraft through the air. It will be less than the ground speed if there is a strong tail wind, more if there is a head wind.

air traffic control Ground control of airplanes in flight, to ensure safety and prevent obstruction.

altimeter An instrument that tells a pilot his height above sea level.

altitude Height above sea level.

apron Hard-surface area of airport used for parking and loading aircraft.

astronautics The science or art of space travel.

artificial horizon An instrument that shows a pilot the "attitude" of his aircraft in relation to the horizon.

autogiro An aircraft which has rotary wings similar to those of a helicopter, but which also has a powered propeller mounted as in an ordinary airplane. The rotary wings are not powered, but turn in the slipstream.

autoland Automatic systems that make it possible for an aircraft to land "blind."

automatic pilot Mechanism for flying a plane automatically when set by the pilot or by ground control.

autopilot *See* AUTOMATIC PILOT.

aviation Flight by heavier-than-air machines.

B

balloon A lighter-than-air aircraft consisting of a basket attached to a large gas-filled bag.

banking The tilting of an aircraft when turning.

beacon *See* RADIO BEACON.

biplane An aircraft with an upper and a lower wing.

black box *See* FLIGHT RECORDER.

bomber A warplane designed for making bombing raids into enemy territory.

C

cabin The passenger compartment of an airliner, or the passenger and pilot compartment of a light aircraft.

canard The tail-first design of some early airplanes. Some modern high-speed airplanes also have a small canard wing at the front.

cantilever wing A wing without any outside bracing wires or other supports.

cockpit The pilot's compartment in early aircraft. The term is still used in relation to military planes. *See* FLIGHT DECK.

composite aircraft Two airplanes—one large, one small—designed to operate together. The large plane carries the small one into the air, and then launches it for independent flight.

control column An aircraft control that works the ailerons and elevators.

D

de-icer Equipment for preventing an aircraft's wings and other surfaces from becoming coated with ice—once a frequent cause of crashes.

delta wing The triangular wing used on some high-speed aircraft. Many delta-wing aircraft have no tailplanes.

dihedral Upward or downward slope of an aircraft's wing or wings from the aircraft body to the wing tips. It aids stability in some circumstances.

dirigible An airship that can be steered.

dive bomber A bomber designed for diving on its target and releasing its bombs at a low altitude.

dog fight An aerial combat between fighter planes from opposing sides in war time.

doppler A navigational aid that tells the pilot his ground speed and direction.

drag The air's resistance to the movement of an aircraft through it. Drag is reduced by streamlining.

drift The sideways "sliding" of an aircraft, usually caused by air currents.

droop nose An aircraft nose that can be "drooped" (bent downward) so as not to obstruct the pilot's view when landing.

E

ejector seat A pilot-operated safety device in some high-speed airplanes. If the plane is about to crash, the device shoots the pilot clear so that he can parachute safely to earth.

elevator A hinged flap on the tailplane of an aircraft, used for putting the aircraft into a climb or a dive.

elevon A control flap that acts as both aileron and elevator in a delta-wing aircraft.

F

fail-safe As a safety measure, the provision of a second device or mechanism to take over if the first one fails. Most aircraft have two or three sets of control mechanisms.

fighter A small warplane designed for combat with enemy warplanes.

fin The vertical section of an airplane's tailplane. It helps to keep the aircraft stable. The fin includes the rudder. *See* RUDDER.

fixed-wing airplane An ordinary airplane, as opposed to a helicopter (which has rotating wings) or a swing-wing airplane.

flap A hinged surface on the trailing edge of a wing. It is used to reduce landing speed.

flight deck The control cabin of an airliner, where the pilots, navigator, and flight engineer sit. *See* COCKPIT.

flight plan Information given by an aircraft's pilot to air traffic control authorities about a flight he intends to make. It includes his proposed route, speed, and altitude.

flight recorder A device that automatically records details of an aircraft's flight. It is also known as a "black box." In the event of an accident, the recorded information helps investigators to discover the cause.

flying boat An aircraft that takes off from—and lands on—water. Unlike a seaplane, it lands on its fuselage, which is boat-like in shape. *See* SEAPLANE.

fuselage The body of an aircraft, excluding the wings and the tailplane.

G

glide path An aircraft's approach path to an airport runway in preparation for landing.

glider A fixed-wing, unpowered aircraft. It has to be launched into the air, but can then glide or soar.

ground controller A person who directs aircraft movements from the ground, usually by the use of radio and radar.

gyroplane An aircraft with rotary wings that turn in the slipstream. It is usually called an *autogiro*. See AUTOGIRO.

H

hangar A building in which aircraft are parked.

helicopter An aircraft with powered rotating wings or blades. These rotors or wings provide lift and also propel the aircraft in the desired direction.

high-wing airplane A monoplane with a wing that extends across the top of the fuselage.

holding pattern The flight course of an aircraft waiting for permission to land at an airport. Usually the aircraft is instructed to fly on an oval path.

I

IATA The International Air Transport Association is an organization of airline companies. Through it, its members agree on fares, meals in flight, and similar matters.

ICAO The International Civil Aviation Organization is the world controlling body for civil aviators. It is an agency of the United Nations Organization.

ILS *See* INSTRUMENT LANDING SYSTEM.

instrument landing system (ILS) A method of controlling an aircraft's landing at an airport, using radar and beacons. The aircraft flies down a radar "path" in line with the runway. Instruments tell the pilot whether he is holding the correct course.

J

jet propulsion A method of powering an aircraft using a jet engine. Expanding gas is forced out through a jet pipe or nozzle, and an opposite force propels the aircraft forward.

jetstream A current of fast-flowing air that circles the world at high altitudes. Pilots can sometimes use it to shorten the time of their flights.

jumbo jet A popular name for some big jet airliners.

K L

kite The earliest of heavier-than-air flying devices. A kite flies for the same reason an airplane does, the pull on the string providing the thrust.

launching pad The place from which a rocket takes off.

leading edge The front edge of an airplane wing or of some other airfoil. *See* TRAILING EDGE.

lift The upward force that keeps an aircraft in the air. It results from the passage of air over the wing. *See* AIRFOIL.

loop An aerobatic maneuver in which an aircraft makes a complete vertical circle in the air, returning to its starting point. At the top of the circle, the aircraft is flying upside-down.

low-wing airplane A monoplane with a wing that extends under the fuselage.

M

Mach number A measurement of the speed of an aircraft in relation to the speed of sound. The speed of sound is known as *Mach 1*.

maneuver In aviation, a change of direction by an aircraft in flight. Usually, the term is used for complicated changes.

marker *See* RADIO BEACON.

markings An aircraft's identification letters and other symbols. A civil aircraft has an international civil aircraft marking and a registration index. A military plane has markings indicating its nationality and its military unit.

mid-wing airplane A monoplane with a wing that extends through the middle of the fuselage.

mock-up A full-scale model of an aircraft built in the early stages of design. A mock-up does not fly, and is constructed only to help with basic design problems and to give a general picture of the proposed aircraft.

monocoque A hollow structure without bracing. The structure is designed to withstand stresses without the need for extra support. The fuselage of all modern aircraft is of monocoque construction. In early aircraft, the fuselage was braced with many internal wires and struts.

monoplane An airplane with only one wing, extending on each side of the fuselage. Most modern aircraft are monoplanes.

montgolfière A hot-air balloon, named after the brothers Joseph and Étienne Montgolfier, who made the first hot-air balloon in 1783.

mooring tower The mast to which airships are moored.

multiplane An airplane with more than three wings. Few such aircraft have been built.

N

nacelle Any "bump" or compartment on the outside of an aircraft, such as an engine housing or a housing for special equipment.

navigation lights Lights carried by an aircraft at night to signal its presence and show the direction in which it is flying. A red light is carried on the port wing tip, a green light on the starboard.

notam Information notice issued by air traffic control authorities.

O P

outrigger A structure supporting parts of an aircraft that are not mounted directly on the fuselage.

overshoot A faulty landing that finishes beyond the end of the runway.

pancake landing A "flop" landing, made at too low a speed and at too steep an angle.

parachute An umbrella-shaped device used to slow down the fall of a person or an object from a height. Using a parachute, a person can, for example, descend safely to Earth from a crashing airplane. Parachutes are also used as brakes to slow down aircraft when landing.

pilot The person who operates the flying controls of an aircraft.

pitch The angle of the blades of a propeller or rotating wing to the air.

pitching See-saw or rocking-horse movement by an aircraft in flight.

precision approach radar A radar system that provides exact information guiding an aircraft during landing.

pressurization A system for maintaining normal pressure inside an aircraft even at high altitudes. Without it, passengers would experience extreme discomfort.

propeller A rotating shaft with long spiral blades used for propelling some airplanes. In the past nearly all aircraft had propellers, but today most have jet propulsion.

pusher propeller A propeller mounted at the rear of its engine, so that it "pushes" the aircraft rather than "pulls" it.

R

radial engine A piston engine in which the cylinders are arranged in a circle around the crankshaft.

radio beacon A radio transmitting device on the ground that tells a pilot whether he is on the correct line of approach to a runway.

reverse thrust Directing the thrust of a jet engine forward to slow down an aircraft when landing.

roll An aerobatic maneuver in which an aircraft makes a complete sideways roll. Half-way through the roll, it is upside-down.

rotary wing The rotating wing of a helicopter. It provides lift and thrust. It is also called a *rotor*.

rotorcraft A helicopter or a gyroplane.

rudder The hinged portion of an aircraft's fin. It is moved to turn the aircraft to left or right.

runway The concrete or asphalt "road" on which an aircraft lands at an airport.

S

sailplane A glider designed for long-distance or long-duration flight.

seaplane An aircraft designed to take off from—and land on—water. Its undercarriage has floats instead of wheels. See FLYING BOAT.

sesquiplane A biplane with one wing much smaller than the other.

short take-off and landing See STOL.

simulator A replica flight deck used in training pilots.

slipstream The stream of air driven backward by the propeller of an airplane.

sonic boom A double bang as an aircraft passes the "sound barrier." It is caused by pressure waves.

sound barrier The shaking and bouncing experienced by an aircraft as it approaches the speed of sound.

spin An aerobatic maneuver in which an aircraft falls vertically while spinning around. In the early days of flying, spins were accidental and almost always fatal.

SST Supersonic transport—that is, supersonic airliners.

stall A rapid loss of height by an aircraft because of loss of lift.

STOL Short take-off and landing. An aircraft designed to operate from relatively short runways. STOL aircraft include swing-wing airplanes.

supersonic flight Flight at above the speed of sound (Mach 1).

swing-wing airplane Aircraft with wings that can be altered in shape during flight, for better performance. They are also called *variable geometry* aircraft.

T

test pilot A pilot who test-flies new aircraft.

thermal A rising current of air used by gliders in soaring.

thrust The force driving an aircraft forward.

trailing edge The rear edge of an airplane wing or of some other airfoil. See LEADING EDGE.

triplane An aircraft with three wings.

turbofan A turbojet engine with a fan that increases the flow of air.

turbojet The standard form of jet engine.

turboprop A jet engine that drives a propeller as well as providing jet propulsion.

UVW

undercarriage An aircraft's landing gear.

variable geometry See SWING-WING AIRPLANE.

vertical take-off and landing See VTOL.

VTOL Vertical take-off and landing. A fixed-wing aircraft designed to take off vertically into the air, and then to fly as a normal airplane.

weather briefing The meteorological information given to a pilot before he starts a flight. It tells him the type of weather he may expect over his route.

wing The main airfoil of an aircraft. The part of the aircraft that produces lift.

wingspan The length of an aircraft's wing, from wingtip to wingtip.

IMPORTANT DATES IN AVIATION HISTORY

1783 In Paris, the first persons to "fly," J. F. Pilâtre de Rozier and the Marquis d'Arlandes, ascended in a captive Montgolfier hot-air balloon (October). Later (November), they made a 5-mile (8-km) balloon flight across the city.

1785 John Jeffries and Jean-Pierre Blanchard made the first crossing of the English Channel, in a balloon. It was also the first international flight.

1852 In Paris, Henri Giffard made the first controlled flight. His craft was a steam-powered airship.

1903 Orville Wright made the first controlled and sustained flight in a powered airplane, at Kitty Hawk, North Carolina. He and his brother Wilbur tossed a coin for the honor of making the flight.

1905 Orville Wright made the first airplane flight of over half an hour.

1909 Louis Blériot made the first airplane crossing of the English Channel. The airplane's possibilities in war cause concern.

1910 Henri Fabre made the first flight in a seaplane.

1911 During the Italo-Turkish war, the Italians made the first use of airplanes in warfare.

1912 In the United States, the French pilot Jules Védrines made the first flight of more than 100 mph.

1912 An American, Capt. Albert Berry, made the first parachute descent from an airplane.

1914 The world's first scheduled passenger service began, between St. Petersburg and Tampa, Florida.

1915 The first all-metal airplane was built in Germany. It was called the Junkers J1.

1918 In Britain, the first true aircraft carrier, HMS *Argus*, was completed.

1919 Capt. John Alcock and Lieut. Arthur Whitten Brown made the first non-stop crossing of the Atlantic. They flew from Newfoundland to the west coast of Ireland.

1923 Juan de la Cierva's Autogyro made the first flight by a rotary-wing aircraft. The flight was made in Madrid.

1927 Charles Lindbergh (the *Lone Eagle*) made the first solo transatlantic flight. He flew from Mineola, NY, to Paris, where he received a hero's welcome.

1929 The German airship *Graf Zeppelin* made the first flight around the world. It took 21 days.

1932 Amelia Earhart made the first woman's transatlantic solo, from Newfoundland to Ireland in about 15 hours. She was idolized by millions of Americans.

1933 The American Wiley Post made the first around-the-world solo flight. His plane was the Lockheed Vega *Winnie Mae*. He took nearly 8 days.

1937 Amelia Earhart lost in Pacific in around-the-world flight. Her disappearance remains a mystery.

1939 The world's first jet flight was made by a German monoplane, the Heinkel He 178. It reached a speed of 435 mph (700 kph).

1947 A Bell X-1 rocket-powered airplane, piloted by Capt. Charles E. Yeager, USAF, became the first aircraft to exceed the speed of sound in level flight. It reached a speed of 670 mph (1,078 kph). The X-1 was air-launched: it was carried into the air by a B-29 bomber.

1949 The first non-stop around-the-world flight was made by Capt. James Gallagher, USAF, and a crew of 13 in a B-50 Superfortress. The plane was refuelled in the air four times.

1956 The first flight at more than 1,000 mph was made by Peter Twiss in a Fairey Delta 2.

1976 A Lockheed SR-71A set an air speed record of 2,193 mph (3,529 kph).